# Dear Old Nebraska U

University of Nebraska Press | Lincoln

# DEAR OLD NEBRASKA U

## CELEBRATING 150 YEARS

University of Nebraska–Lincoln with Kim Hachiya

Craig Chandler, Director of Photography

Foreword by Ted Kooser

Library of Congress Control Number: 2018959950
Set in ITC New Baskerville.

# Contents

GRIT

GLORY

# A Message from Chancellor Ronnie Green

*Dear Old Nebraska U.*

As I peruse the pages of this inspiring book—150 years of the University of Nebraska–Lincoln's history told through 150 people, places, and events—I am struck by how much this University has accomplished in its relatively young 150 years. From the stark 1869 photo of Lincoln's few scattered houses and University Hall towering above the prairie landscape (page xvi), to the panoramic view of the modern City Campus, replete with new buildings rising from the skyline (page 1), the remarkable ways that our University has grown and flourished is clear. The University of Nebraska–Lincoln has become an essential and vital link to the state, the region, the nation, and the world. It is, indeed, in the middle of everywhere and everything. From the founders who dreamed of a home on the prairie for higher education and research; to the untold number of dedicated faculty, administrators, and staff, past and present; to the thousands of students and all of our alumni; and to everyone else who has invested intellectually, financially, or spiritually to make the University of Nebraska what it is today: we share pieces of our story here.

More important, we are preparing the University for the next 150 years. This book celebrates 150 phenomenal years of our University and recognizes the actions and vision of people throughout this century and a half who have positioned us to continue moving forward.

The future is possible only by acknowledging and building on the past—and the University of Nebraska–Lincoln has a solid foundation to build on. We are excited about and committed to the future: delivering the best student experience in the Big Ten, attracting a larger and increasingly diverse student population, and growing the impact of world-leading research endeavors and creative activities by continuing to attract excellent faculty and students at all levels and in all disciplines. Proud of our heritage as a land grant university, we are also dedicated to improving the lives of people in our state and nation, and, indeed, around the world. How do we do this? By being at the forefront of research in food and water security, in human healthcare design and delivery, and in bioengineering (particularly in relation to national defense and well-being); by being a leader in early childhood development and education; by recognizing our position at the vanguard of developments in emerging media and technology; by continuing our commitment to the arts and humanities through excellent endeavors such as our Center for Digital Research in the Humanities and our world-class museums on campus. The future is a bright one. I can only imagine that for our 175th anniversary it will be difficult to tell our story in just 175 entries.

I am sure that, like me, you will enjoy paging through this wonderful book, looking for and finding many of the things that are dear to you about your university. I invite you to do it often. I know you'll discover many stories to make you proud of the University of Nebraska—both our history and our future. *Dear Old Nebraska U.*

N
GO B1G RED
NEBRASKA
NEBRASKA HUSKERS

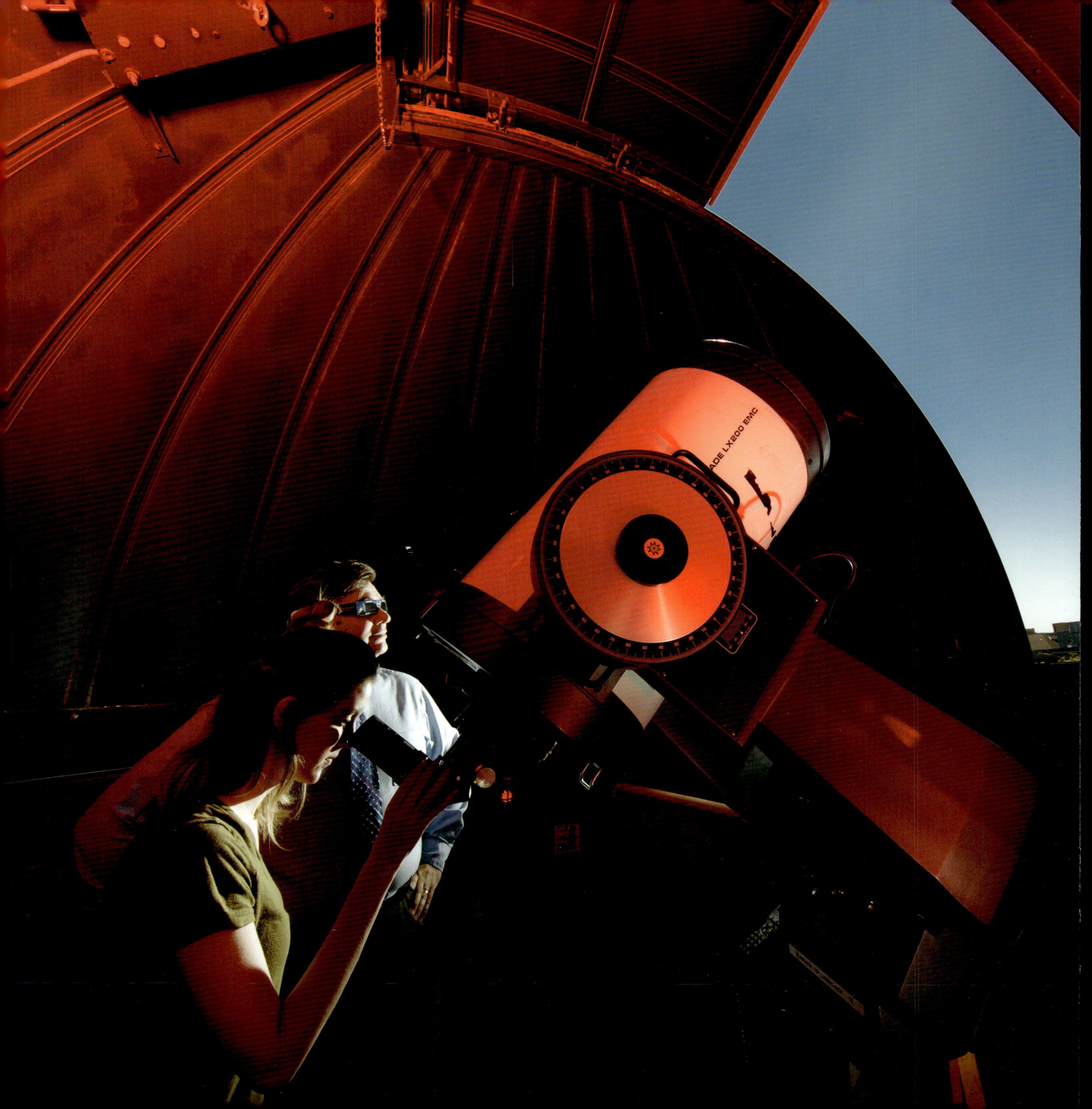
ADE LX200 EMC

# Foreword by Ted Kooser

## AN INVITATION

When I was a very little boy my parents enrolled me in a nursery school supervised by the Home Economics Department at Iowa State University. I remember nothing of this, but my uncle, who was in charge of a university service that provided films and projectors for classroom use, made a 16-mm film of me playing with other children in a fenced outdoor enclosure surrounded by serious-looking young women, some standing at the fence, some seated on folding chairs, taking notes on our behavior. That was my first experience with higher education. It seems quaint today, but it's still how we learn from one another. We make our notes and then we think about them. In that flickering black-and-white film one can see various playthings set out for the children to pick up and move, to climb on and over, and somewhere in the past are some hurriedly handwritten notes on what Teddy Kooser, so cute despite oversized ears, picked up to throw at some hapless little boy or girl.

My experience with universities has continued for more than seventy years. As of the date of this writing I am a part-time professor of creative writing at the university that is the subject of this wonderful book of short essays and photographs.

Though I worked for many years at a life insurance company in Lincoln, I was only three blocks from City Campus and I spent many lunch hours walking through the gardens south of Love Library, through Morrill Hall among the bones of the ages, and climbing the airy open stairs of Sheldon Memorial Art Gallery to see what I might find—all additions to the catalog of experiences being jotted down in longhand by those home ec majors of three-quarters of a century before.

Leafing through this handsome commemorative book has made me think about the notion of a university. The root of "university," of course, is "universe," which suggests that it contains everything. Well, perhaps not *everything,* but what of everything is known, the multifold planets and stars and dark matter and all of the knowledge and experience we've gathered in the past few thousand years, as well as what we'll likely learn tomorrow and the next day and the next. It is in that sense a grand museum, and we are all invited in.

Our university is a place where everyone is encouraged to be an individual, and yet all of us are gathered together in this great museum our state has provided, often walking from classroom to classroom in a state of anxious wonder, sometimes deliriously happy. Here's something I saw one morning, walking to Andrews Hall:

> 6:30 a.m., dark, still, and cold, and members of the marching band in down-filled jackets, stocking caps, and mittens, carrying instruments in cases black as dominoes, or bellying great moony drums, or shouldering tubas, free hands pinching folders stuffed with music, trudge toward the stadium, not one among them talking to another, each walking sullen and apart, all sleepy, stumbly, slightly sour, each one a little part of something soon to be put together under the banks of lights already burning over a field as green as antifreeze, soon to be making their enormous, joyful, rumbling, brassy, honking, rattling, calamitous fanfare, rolling around and around the echoing bowl like a ball in roulette, a crash of sound right in the quiet intersection of night and morning . . .

A university is a universe of experiences, and that wonderful coming together of people with a common end in sight is, I think, what happens here.

# Introduction

What sparks the desire to open a university on a grassy prairie in a town that barely exists? Is it hubris? Desire to compete? The chance to take advantage of "free land and money"? The need to prove legitimacy? Hope and optimism? Perhaps all these and more.

Even before Nebraska was granted statehood in 1867, its territorial residents were planning for schools and colleges; education symbolized success and an eye toward the future. On February 15, 1869, taking advantage of the federal Morrill Land-Grant Act of 1862, the bill establishing the University of Nebraska unanimously passed both houses of the Nebraska Legislature. Governor David Butler signed the bill into law the same day.

The Morrill Act granted to the states land, wrested either by treaty or force from indigenous people, that could be sold or leased to provide funds for universities. States had just three years from statehood to accept provisions of the act, and only two more years to construct a building and open a university. Nebraska met both deadlines.

Almost immediately the University was beset by problems. There were differences over what coursework the University should offer. There were budget issues. There was a significant lack of population from which to draw students, and those students were underprepared for college-level work. The first building erected on the new campus was ill conceived and dreadfully constructed. And the four city blocks reserved for the University sat along the banks of a creek that often flooded. Despite these challenges, on January 7, 1871, the University regents hired Allen Benton, president of Mount Union College in Ohio, as the University of Nebraska's first chancellor. Benton arrived that summer and immediately began promoting the University across the state. He also hired four men to become the University's first faculty.

Benton designed the University's official seal, which features an open book in the center surrounded by the Latin phrase "*Literis Dedicata et Omnibus Artibus*," that is, "Dedicated to Letters and All the Arts." The seal includes symbols of the schools and colleges Benton hoped would eventually comprise the University: agriculture, law, mechanical engineering, civil engineering, military, medicine, and fine arts.

When the doors of the University of Nebraska opened in the fall of 1871, the majority of the 130 students were enrolled in the college preparatory Latin School; just 20 pursued University coursework. In spring 1873 the University produced its first two graduates, with three more graduating in 1874. There were no graduates in 1875, but five earned baccalaureate degrees in 1876, including the first woman; two master's degrees also were conferred that year.

Nebraskans of 1869 could not have imagined the University of 2019. The modern University of Nebraska—now with facilities in all ninety-three counties, around 26,000 students, and nearly 7,000 employees—is remarkably different from that early university. The school originally focused solely on educating students; the ideas of research and outreach to citizens were not envisioned, but both have become part of Nebraska's tripartite mission of teaching and learning, research and discovery, and outreach and service.

From humble beginnings Nebraska has become a university that houses a laser that is more powerful than ten thousand suns. Improvements in seeds, agricultural practices, and irrigation advanced by research at the University has greatly increased crop yields across the globe. Nebraska innovators have developed new meat products that are safer for consumers, while methods for preventing and ameliorating brain damage from concussions are under study. Young children are better ready for school thanks to Nebraska research on rural education, and Nebraska is a leader in digital research in the humanities. The University is the state's largest employer and graduates more students into the workforce than any other institution in Nebraska.

Built on optimism and promise, determination and resilience, the University of Nebraska celebrates its first 150 years and looks to a future of progress and triumph. In our grit, our glory.

UNIVERSITAS NEBRASKENSIS.
FEB. 15, 1869.
LITERIS DEDICATA ET OMNIBUS ARTIBUS

# Dear Old Nebraska U

# One University

## TEACHING, RESEARCH, AND SERVICE

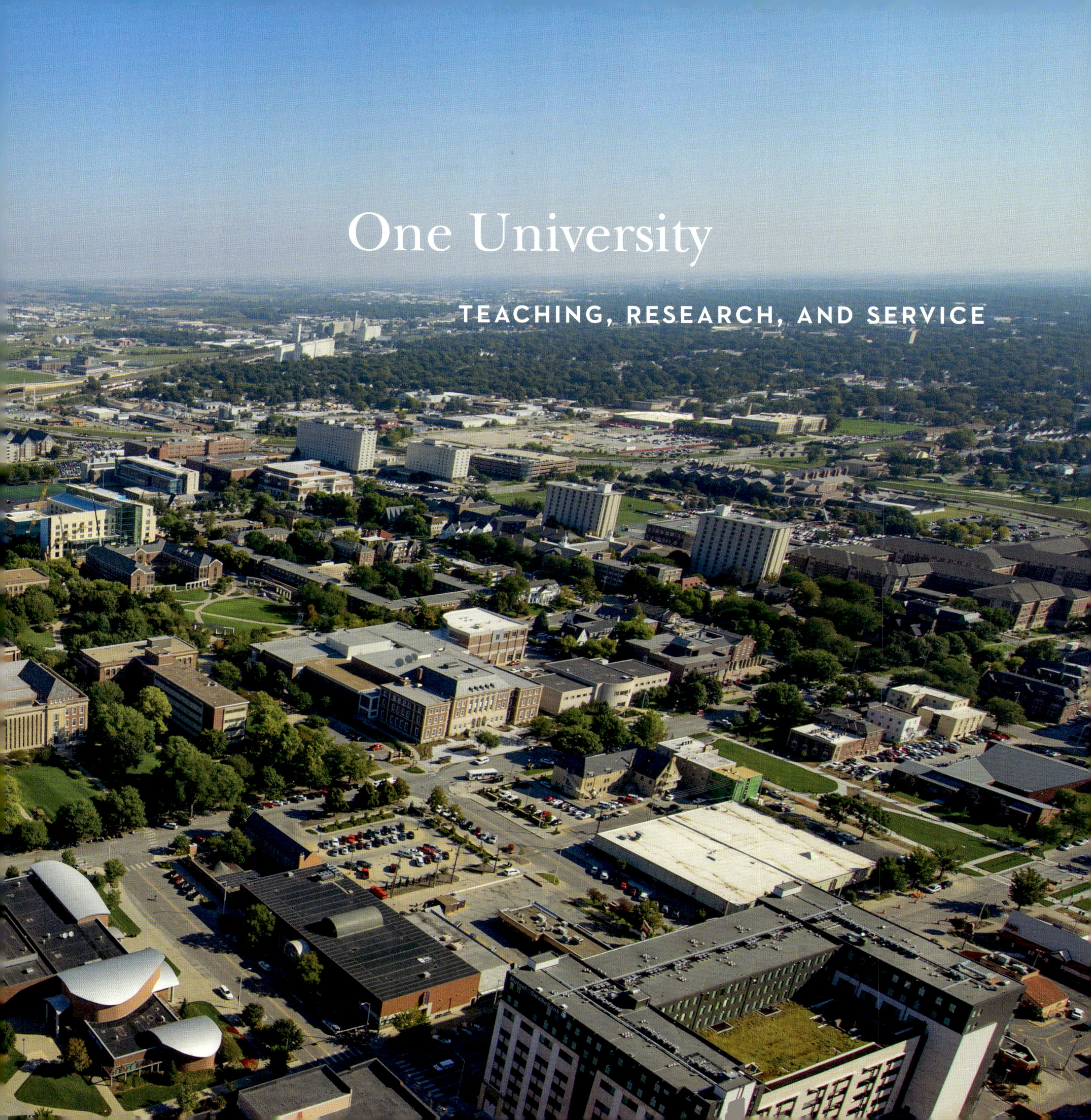

IN OUR GRIT, OUR GLORY

The charter establishing the University of Nebraska provided for six colleges: agriculture, law, mechanical engineering, civil engineering, military, medicine, and fine arts. The University opened with only one functioning college—Literature, Science and the Arts—and students were taught a prescribed curriculum across a smattering of subject areas, but primarily the classics. Today the University of Nebraska–Lincoln is home to ten colleges offering well over one hundred majors and countless courses from which students can choose.

The University's service and outreach mission was developed through the establishment of experiment stations and later Nebraska Extension. The University embraces its responsibility to extend its resources beyond the boundaries of campus with facilities spread across the state.

The economic and cultural impact of the University on the state is significant and far-reaching, from sustaining a highly skilled workforce to training future leaders in fields such as agriculture, engineering, and business, to producing innovative global solutions through research for solving the unique challenges facing the state. The value of a high-quality education is priceless, and Nebraska students establish a lifelong connection to the Cornhusker State.

The University touches lives and communities across the state, the nation, and the world. Development of new knowledge, processes, and discoveries through research and creative activity, as well as leadership and engagement by faculty, staff, and students, together improve lives and well-being globally.

The University is focused on the future, with the colleges and campuses embodying the power of ideas in action, of people striving to improve the world. Together we are the University of Nebraska.

## The Charter

Written by Nebraska state legislator Augustus Harvey in 1869, the charter of the University of Nebraska lays out the governance and guiding principles of the University. The charter provided for the establishment of six colleges and states that the University's purpose is "to afford to the inhabitants of this State the means of acquiring a thorough knowledge of the various branches of literature, science and the arts." Notably, section 18 of the charter affirms: "No person shall, because of age, sex, color, or nationality be deprived of the privileges of this institution." Control of the University was placed in the hands of twelve regents, nine of whom were elected by the Nebraska Legislature; the remaining three were the governor, the state superintendent of public instruction, and the chancellor. The charter is housed in the Archives and Special Collections of the University of Nebraska–Lincoln Libraries, a part of the handwritten and red leather–bound minutes of the first meeting of the University of Nebraska Board of Regents.

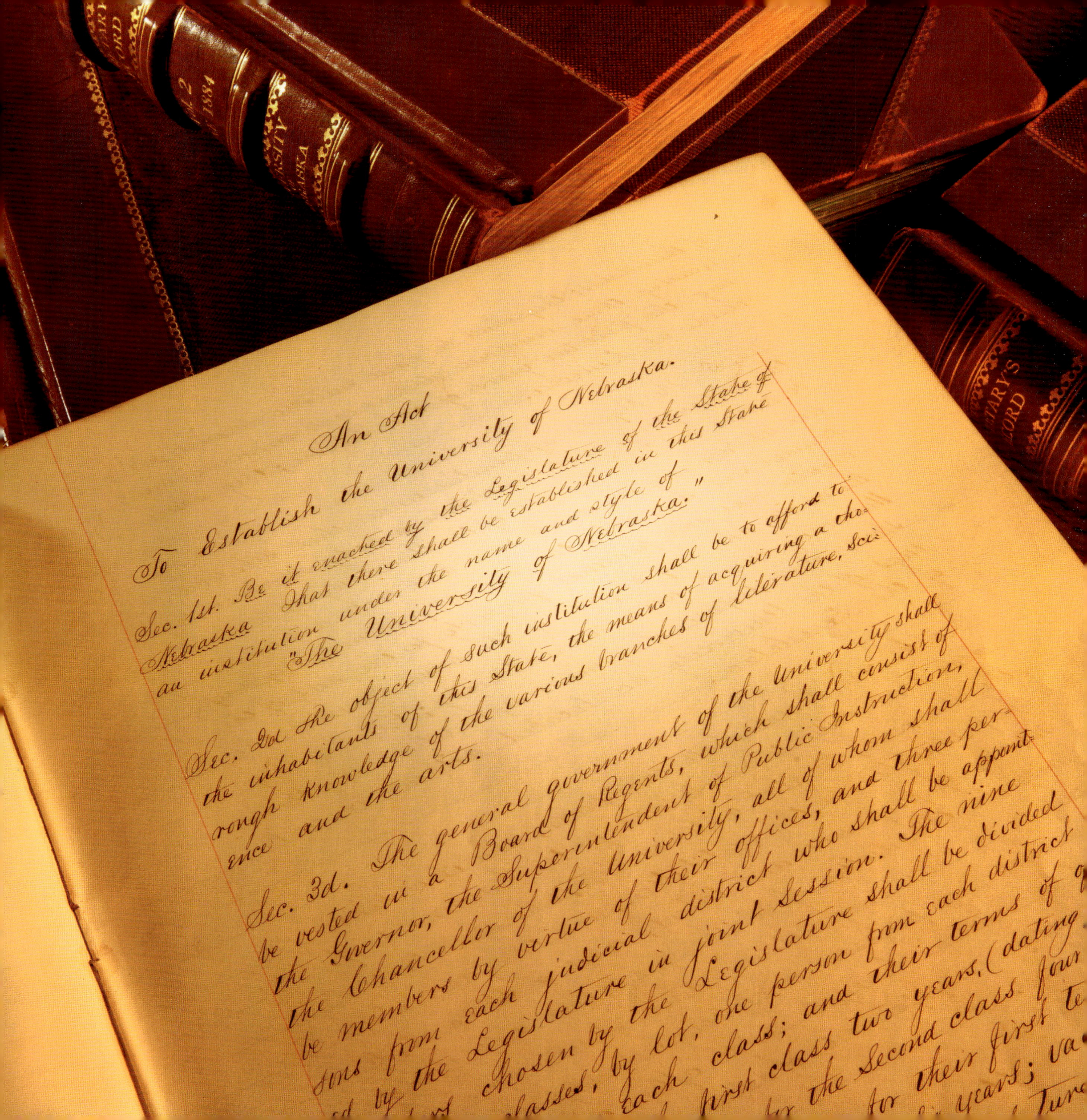

An Act
To Establish the University of Nebraska.
Sec. 1st. Be it enacted by the Legislature of the State of
Nebraska That there shall be established in this State
an institution under the name and style of
"The University of Nebraska."
Sec. 2d The object of such institution shall be to afford to
the inhabitants of this State, the means of acquiring a tho-
rough knowledge of the various branches of literature, Sci-
ence and the arts.
Sec. 3d. The general government of the University shall
be vested in a Board of Regents, which shall consist of
the Governor, the Superintendent of Public Instruction,
the Chancellor of the University, all of whom shall
be members by virtue of their offices, and three per-
sons from each judicial district who shall be appoint-
ed by the Legislature in joint Session. The nine
chosen by the Legislature shall be divided
classes, by lot, one person from each district
each class; and their terms of
first class two years, (dating
the Second class four
for their first

## College of Arts and Sciences

The College of Ancient and Modern Literature, Mathematics and the Natural Sciences opened in fall 1871 as the first college at Nebraska. It was never known by its formal name and instead came to be known as the College of Literature, Science and the Arts. Today's College of Arts and Sciences is the school's largest college, enrolling more than 4,000 undergraduates and close to 1,000 graduate students, with more than 45,000 alumni. Its nearly 800 faculty and staff are aligned in fifty-nine departments, centers, programs, and institutes. The college offers thirty-four majors and fifty-nine minors, ranging from actuarial science to Great Plains studies, biochemistry to philosophy, and economics to sociology. In 2018 the college launched a new funding initiative to encourage the formation of mutually beneficial collaborations between its faculty and organizations outside of the University in order to fuel innovation, address societal issues, and contribute to the public good.

The college includes research initiatives like the NIMBUS (Nebraska Intelligent MoBile Unmanned Systems) Lab, which combines software and systems engineering with robotics research and technology to develop more capable and dependable unmanned vehicles. The Nebraska Center for Materials and Nanoscience, founded in 1988, is a nationally recognized center of excellence in materials research science and engineering, nanoscience, and nanotechnology. Among the college's many initiatives are the Institute for Ethnic Studies, established in 1972—which offers three interdisciplinary programs of study and supports student organizations like the Mexican American Student Association, the University of Nebraska Inter-Tribal Exchange, and the Afrikan Peoples Union—and the Women's and Gender Studies Program, formed in 1976.

## College of Agricultural Sciences and Natural Resources

The Agriculture Department, organized in 1872, is the second-oldest college at Nebraska. The University's own Charles Bessey wrote the pertinent sections of the federal Hatch Act, passed in 1887, which defined the role of agricultural education and science. Bessey created the idea of the experiment station, where research and experimentation could be conducted. The linkage of experiment stations and land grant universities was critical, and the Hatch Act provided federal money to support agricultural science. Bessey's work led to the construction of Agriculture Hall in 1904 and the layout of an agriculture campus east of the University's main campus, today's East Campus.

Today's College of Agricultural Sciences and Natural Resources is part of the Institute of Agriculture and Natural Resources and most of the college's units are located on Nebraska's East Campus. The college enrolls more than 2,000 undergraduates and 700 graduates in thirty-three programs and has produced nearly 20,000 alumni. Areas of study span animal, plant, and human health and well-being, earth systems analysis, agricultural production and processing, global climate change, agricultural market structures, water resources, and land-use change. CASNR's programs prepare students for an array of careers in production agriculture, international business, and natural resources management. The unique Engler Agribusiness Entrepreneurship Program enables select students to grow an idea into an enterprise.

The college remains true to its historic roots, applying science to practice. Recent research has led to the development of the flat iron steak from beef cattle, and much of the wheat grown in Nebraska comes from seed developed in UNL labs.

## College of Law

The University's original seal and charter both indicate the intention for a College of Law at Nebraska; the college was eventually established in 1891 when the University acquired the private Central College of Law. Classes originally met in University Hall but in 1911 the state legislature provided for a new building at 10th and R Streets. The college occupied this building until 1975, when it moved to East Campus. Since 2001 the college has invested nearly $12 million in a complete renovation of its facilities. The college has nearly 400 students and more than 30 faculty. Notable initiatives include Space, Cyber, and Telecommunications law; a number of joint-degree programs; and the Children's Justice Clinic, which prepares lawyers to serve as advocates for children entangled in the justice system.

The University of Nebraska College of Law has more than 9,000 alumni, including five former governors, fifty presidents of state bar associations, and many senior partners in law firms nationwide.

## Graduate Studies

In 1876 UNL conferred its first graduate degrees upon two men, who in 1873 earned the first bachelor's degrees from UNL. Faculty and administrators believed graduate-level study would help maintain Nebraska's place among other educational institutions, and faculty developed other courses of study, such as the Botanical Seminar, known as Sem. Bot., which graduated some of the nation's most famous botanists of the era.

In 1896 the Board of Regents formally approved the organization of the Graduate College and Nebraska became the first major institution west of the Mississippi to organize a graduate school. The program was unusual in that it conferred degrees based upon a student's body of research and the quality of that research as opposed to the then more common method of conferring degrees based on time spent in a program. Current graduate enrollment at Nebraska is nearly 4,500.

## College of Engineering

The College of Engineering was originally part of the Industrial College, which incorporated both agriculture and engineering. Eventually the two programs separated into distinct entities, and an act of the legislature officially established the College of Engineering in 1909. The sole college of engineering in the state, the College of Engineering offers academic programs on three campuses in two cities: City Campus and East Campus in Lincoln and Scott Campus in Omaha. Combined, the college has more than 22,000 alumni. Over 3,000 undergraduates and nearly 500 graduate students are currently enrolled, taught by 175 faculty.

In addition to the Durham School of Architectural Engineering and Construction, the college's offerings include biological systems engineering, chemical and biomolecular engineering, civil engineering, computer science and engineering, electrical and computer engineering, and mechanical and materials engineering. Nebraska engineering graduates are solving problems related to water pollution and the restoration of streams, lakes, and wetlands; they are developing new uses for bioproducts and bioenergy, from biodiesel and ethanol research to new uses for grain by-products; and they are improving food safety and quality. Nebraska civil engineers design buildings and bridges, protect water and air quality, build transportation systems, develop construction materials, and manage water resources.

Along with private donations, the college has received a $70 million allocation from the State of Nebraska to renovate and build new facilities, including new and expanded lab space that will accommodate increased enrollments.

## College of Architecture

The first formal courses in architecture at UNL were offered in 1894. As the discipline became more established professionally, Nebraska created an architecture department in 1930, which formalized into the College of Engineering and Architecture in 1964. The distinct College of Architecture was established in 1973. The college's first chair, appointed in 1930, had worked with Bertram Goodhue, the architect of Nebraska's acclaimed State Capitol Building. Since the beginning the architecture curriculum has blended the arts and aesthetics of buildings with technical and scientific engineering principles.

The college has a six-year professional sequence that culminates in a master of architecture degree, as well as undergraduate programs in architecture, interior design, and landscape architecture and a graduate program in community and regional planning. The college's 44 faculty members guide the studies of nearly 400 undergraduate students, over 40 graduate students, and nearly 90 professional students. Among the college's unique initiatives is Design Health, a collaborative, interdisciplinary program that addresses the design needs of healthcare facilities, from the largest hospitals to the smallest clinics around the globe. The college has more than 4,000 alumni working worldwide.

## College of Business

Founded as the School of Commerce in 1913, the College of Business Administration was created in 1919—the University's fiftieth year of operation. Today nearly 4,500 students and 125 faculty are part of the College of Business, which provides ten undergraduate majors, five minors, and two certificate programs. The college is the only PhD-granting business college in the state. The college has produced nearly 40,000 alumni in its first one hundred years.

The college is housed in Howard L. Hawks Hall, which opened in 2017 and includes the Husker Shop, a learning partnership between Nebraska Athletics and sports merchandiser Fanatics. College students manage the shop, and the data from the store is integrated into the curriculums of several business degree majors. In addition, the college's Trading Room, a state-of-the-art simulated stock trading area, provides a real-time environment for students to experience what it is like to work in finance. In spring 2018 the college's master of business administration program vaulted into the Top 20 Best Programs as ranked by *U.S. News and World Report*. The magazine lists Nebraska's MBA program as seventh among Big Ten institutions and thirteenth among all public universities.

The College of Business partners with the Clifton Foundation and Gallup Management and Consulting to oversee the Don Clifton Strengths Institute, which provides training, education, workshops, and coaching on strengths-based leadership; early identification of high-achieving students through the Clifton Builders program; and research support for the college's faculty and students. Donald O. Clifton was a longtime instructor and researcher at UNL who developed the Clifton StrengthsFinder; he served as chairman of Selection Research Inc. and later as chairman of Gallup.

## Nebraska Extension

Nebraska Extension is part of the University's tripartite mission of teaching and learning, research and discovery, and engagement and outreach. Nebraska Extension grew out of the philosophy that the University had something of value to offer to the state's residents. Early in the University's history, "farmer's institutes" were held to disseminate information about the latest research into farming practices. Extension worked to help farmers and ranchers ramp up food production to aid the war effort during World War I and was on the front lines assisting rural Nebraskans in managing the effects of the Great Depression and droughts of the 1930s.

Extension agents, now called extension educators, lead programs in animal agriculture; crops for the future; child, youth, and families; entrepreneurship; food, nutrition, and health; and water and the environment. Nebraska Extension also supports 4-H, which involves more than 144,000 Nebraska youth participants. Through Nebraska Extension the University serves all ninety-three Nebraska counties through eighty-three county offices and four research centers in Scottsbluff, North Platte, Norfolk, and Mead. Extension services are administered through the UNL Institute of Agriculture and Natural Resources.

## Institute of Agriculture and Natural Resources

In 1973 the Nebraska Legislature established the Institute of Agriculture and Natural Resources (IANR) at UNL. The institute was activated after more than a decade of discussions, proposals, and controversies. IANR is a University-wide institution and the only entity within the school's system that offers programs in both agriculture and natural resources. Some 40 percent of IANR faculty and staff are located at research and extension centers and county-based extension offices outside Lincoln. IANR faculty and staff have appointments in the Agricultural Research Division, the College of Agricultural Sciences and Natural Resources, the College of Education and Human Sciences, Nebraska Extension, the Nebraska Forest Service, and the Nebraska Statewide Arboretum.

UNL's School of Natural Resource Sciences was established in 1997 as a cross-campus enterprise spanning both the Institute of Agriculture and Natural Resources and the College of Arts and Sciences. When the Conservation and Survey Division was merged with the Water Center in 2003, the School of Natural Resource Sciences became the School of Natural Resources (SNR). SNR faculty, staff, and students come from many fields of study, including ecology, climate science, geography, geology, soil science, water science, and the social sciences. SNR has expanded to include over 150 faculty and staff and nearly 500 undergraduate and graduate students. The school focuses on a variety of initiatives, including increasing understanding of the potential impacts of climate variability and change on natural resources and agricultural productivity, improving water consumption and conservation practices, and enhancing understanding of human-environment interaction.

## College of Journalism and Mass Communications

The University's first journalism class was taught in 1894, and the School of Journalism was originally established in 1923 within the College of Arts and Sciences; it separated from the College of Arts and Sciences in 1979 and was elevated to the College of Journalism in 1985, changing its name to the College of Journalism and Mass Communications in the early 1990s. The college is housed in Harold and Marian Andersen Hall, named after two UNL alumni and donors who have worked tirelessly to insure a free press around the world.

The college enrolls more than 1,000 undergraduates and nearly 70 graduate students. The college boasts Pulitzer Prize and Emmy Award winners among its graduates and faculty and more than 5,000 alumni working in every state and dozens of countries. The college supports an innovative student-run advertising agency and a student-run radio station, KRNU. New initiatives include intensive training in digital media, data-driven reporting, and the use of drones in media. Launched in 2011, Nebraska Mosaic, a community journalism capstone course, has led to the publication of more than 450 stories about Nebraska's refugee and immigrant populations.

Numerous undergraduates have won prestigious national awards for newswriting, advertising, and public relations campaigns and broadcasting projects. In 2017 an in-depth multimedia project, The Wounds of Whiteclay, examined Whiteclay, a tiny Nebraska village bordering the Pine Ridge Indian Reservation of South Dakota, by looking at the toll of alcoholism on the reservation that is fueled by beer sales in the town. The project won the Robert F. Kennedy Journalism Awards grand prize in May 2017 and has been recognized for excellence by the *New York Times* and the *Economist.* It was named among the best global public health stories of 2017 by Johns Hopkins Bloomberg School of Public Health.

## Hixson-Lied College of Fine and Performing Arts

The College of Fine and Performing Arts was established July 1, 1993, encompassing the School of Music, the Department of Art and Art History, and the Department of Theatre Arts and Dance. In recognition of an $18 million gift from Christina M. Hixson and the Lied Foundation Trust, the college was renamed the Hixson-Lied College of Fine and Performing Arts in 2000. The funds support the college and its affiliated programs—the Lied Center for Performing Arts, the Sheldon Museum of Art, the Mary Riepma Ross Media Arts Center, and the Nebraska Repertory Theatre—as well as the Digital Arts Initiative; the Interdisciplinary Arts Symposium; many student grants, graduate fellowships, and undergraduate scholarships; numerous faculty grants and professorships; and the Nebraska Young Artist Awards for talented Nebraska high school juniors. The college has more than 700 undergraduates and nearly 150 graduate students, as well as 105 faculty. The college has produced more than 8,000 alumni.

Three schools comprise the college's academic units: the School of Art, Art History and Design; the Glenn Korff School of Music, named in 2013 in honor of Glenn Korff, a 1956 graduate of the University of Nebraska who provided an $8 million gift to support the school; and the Johnny Carson School of Theatre and Film.

The newest unit, the Johnny Carson Center for Emerging Media Arts, was made possible by a $20 million gift from the Johnny Carson Foundation in 2015. The center focuses on virtual production, film, design, technology, and commerce; students and faculty are able to explore the boundaries of where cinematic storytelling intersects with artificial intelligence, science, humanities, computer science, engineering, music, fine arts, and other disciplines.

## College of Education and Human Sciences

The College of Education and Human Sciences was created in 2003 when Teachers College and the College of Human Resources and Family Sciences became one academic unit. Both colleges have proud histories. Teachers College was formally established on February 14, 1908, to prepare teachers and improve the quality of secondary school teaching by providing courses in history, theory, and the practice of teaching. The School of Domestic Science was established in 1898. Its director, chemistry professor Rosa Bouton, described the curriculum as work "based on scientific principles." The name changed to the Department of Home Economics in 1907; it was re-elevated to be a school in 1962 as part of the College of Agriculture and Home Economics until 1970, when the College of Home Economics became a separate entity. The college includes nearly 3,000 undergraduates, more than 1,000 graduate students, and 263 faculty. The college claims more than 50,000 alumni working in nearly one hundred countries around the globe.

Both colleges are engaged in outreach activities that extend education beyond the classroom. Notable activities include the Robert Hillestad Textiles Gallery; the International Quilt Study Center & Museum; the Buffett Early Childhood Institute; and the Barkley Speech Language and Hearing Clinic. Bullying-prevention strategies, early childhood education, educational psychology, nutrition science, fashion design, and hospitality management are a few of the programs in the college. In addition, the college's focus on early childhood education has positioned it as an international leader in this critical field of study.

## Nebraska Innovation Campus

Nebraska Innovation Campus connects the University with private sector businesses by providing access to research faculty, world-class facilities, and outstanding students. Sited on the former Nebraska State Fairgrounds and adjacent to the north end of City Campus, Innovation Campus aspires to be the most sustainable research and technology campus in the United States by utilizing alternative energy sources, constructing environmentally responsible buildings, and encouraging research in sustainability. Since 2013 offices, conference halls, and lab, pilot plant, and greenhouse space have been completed, housing more than thirty public and private partners. At full build-out the campus will consist of 2.2 million square feet of uniquely designed buildings and amenities that encourage people to create and transform ideas into global innovation. As many as five thousand people will eventually work at Nebraska Innovation Campus, with two-thirds of them working in private businesses. The most visible University tenants to date are the Food Innovation Center, NUtech Ventures (the University's intellectual property and technology commercialization unit), and the Daugherty Water for Food Global Institute.

Innovation Campus's signature building, Innovation Commons, houses a conference center and Nebraska Innovation Studio, Nebraska's largest makerspace. The studio has tools and equipment for use in a range of mediums, from woodworking to ceramics, textiles to design software, and 3D printing and laser cutting. The studio encourages creative thinking, entrepreneurship, and collaboration among institutions and businesses and is open to all in the local community who wish to join.

## University of Nebraska Foundation

Faced with the Depression crisis, University of Nebraska Chancellor Edgar A. Burnett called on thirty business and civic leaders to help establish the University of Nebraska Foundation in 1936. J. C. Seacrest of Lincoln made the first gift to the foundation in memory of his sister, Elizabeth Seacrest Hardy, for support of the construction of a student activity building. In addition to continuous fundraising, the foundation has led three major comprehensive campaigns to sustain the University. The University of Nebraska–Lincoln has benefited immensely from private donations through the years. Every campus area, college, and program has been affected in some way by the philanthropic generosity of its alumni, friends, and member organizations. The foundation has had headquarters in Love Library, Varner Hall, and downtown Lincoln, and it now has offices in Kearney, Lincoln, and Omaha. It is consistently ranked among the top foundations supporting public universities.

## Nebraska Alumni Association

The first Nebraska alumni group was formed in 1874, when the University's first five graduates "organized themselves into an alumni association for purposes of mutual social improvement and the advancement of the . . . University, whose memories and benefits they wish to perpetuate." The first class reunion was held in 1897.

In 1913 the first permanent alumni headquarters was established and the *Nebraska Alumnus* magazine (now *Nebraska Quarterly*) was launched. The association has moved multiple times since its original home in the basement of University Hall and now resides in the Wick Alumni Center.

Over the years the association has expanded the activities offered to alumni, including trips, career resources, the Student Alumni Association, Cather Circle (now the Nebraska Women's Leadership Network), and lifelong learning opportunities. The association currently connects with nearly ninety alumni chapters and affiliate groups and 25,000 individual members around the world, all united by their commitment to supporting the University's future.

GO BIG RED!
GO BIG RED!

N

# Infinite Possibilities

## THE STUDENT EXPERIENCE

GO
RED!
SHOE
SIMON

Of the 130 students enrolled on the University of Nebraska's opening day in 1871, just 20 were university students; the rest were enrolled in the campus's preparatory school. Student housing options were meager—with students living either at home or in boarding- or rooming houses. Social options were limited as well. As the University grew, students began to organize into groups—at first only literary and scientific societies, then later into private Greek-letter organizations and University-operated housing units as well.

Today, student enrollment is around 26,000, with ever-increasing diversity—racial, social, ethnic, cultural, and geographic. More than 10,000 students live on campus, either in residence halls or Greek-letter housing. Husker students can choose from a vast array of campus activities. More than six hundred recognized student organizations operate on campus, with missions ranging from cultural or heritage affiliations to support groups to academic and sporting clubs, including Actuarial Science Club, Zeta Sigma Chi Multicultural Sorority, Biology Club, International Folk Dancers, Competitive Archery Team, and the Soil Judging Team.

While much has changed about campus life since Nebraska's first students entered the classroom, student learning and the student experience remain critical to the University's success. Nebraska faculty, staff, and students are engaged in making student life a bold, distinctive program that defines the unique Nebraska experience. This is more than classroom learning; it involves exploring how housing options (both Greek and residential) impact and affect learning and includes international experiences and service learning opportunities that expand worldviews. It integrates mentorship opportunities and focuses on community building. It reinforces Nebraska's mission and values. It is about becoming a lifelong Husker. For Nebraska students, the future is unlimited.

## Student Success

Nebraska makes significant investments in programs aimed at helping all students realize academic, social, and cultural success during their time on campus. First-year and transfer students attend New Student Enrollment during the summer before beginning classes, where they meet with academic advisors and enroll in first semester courses. The Nebraska First-Year Experience and the Nebraska Transition Program, both of which launched in 2013, provide support for students in and outside the classroom. Academic tutoring and coaching, peer mentoring, workshops, and other activities aim to increase student retention and graduation rates. Thousands of students have benefited from these programs.

Nebraska has twenty-five first-year and three upper-class learning communities that connect students with shared academic interests to classroom and experiential opportunities. Students in learning communities typically live together on the same residence hall floor and have at least one shared class and participate in shared social and professional activities.

Nebraska's academic advisors play a critical role in helping students navigate curriculum requirements and make choices regarding coursework and future careers. Nebraska's Career Services team connects academic curriculum offerings with real-world experiences through major- and career-exploration activities, job shadowing, and internships.

Many programs support students of color and first-generation and low-income students, including the Nebraska College Preparatory Academy, the William H. Thompson Scholars Learning Community, the Emerging Leaders Scholars Program, and the Office of Academic Success and Intercultural Services.

## Commencement

Nebraska's first commencement exercise in 1872 graduated no students but did confer an honorary degree to the Right Rev. Bishop Clarkson of Omaha. At the second commencement the following year, two degrees were awarded, both to men, and the first woman graduated three years later in 1876. In the 1890s a second commencement was added to the calendar to coincide with Charter Day in February. Nebraska graduates and faculty began wearing academic regalia (caps and gowns).

Between 1900 and 1919 many prominent orators delivered the commencement address, including Booker T. Washington, president of Tuskegee Institute; William Jennings Bryan; and President Theodore Roosevelt. The latter was one of ten luminaries to receive honorary degrees during the 1917 commencement that also celebrated the fiftieth anniversary of Nebraska's statehood. Commencement has been held in various locations across campus, both indoors and out, moving to the Devaney Center in 1976 and then to Pinnacle Bank Arena in 2013.

## Charter Day

The University was formally chartered on February 15, 1869, and for many years Charter Day was celebrated on that anniversary. Charter Day included various festivities, including sports competitions, alumni meetings, speakers, open houses hosted by each of the colleges, and—for a few decades, at least—winter commencement. It is unclear when Charter Day ceased as a tradition, though it was likely in the late 1950s. Ivy Day eclipsed Charter Day in importance for students, though by the 1970s it too had faded from being an all-University event to one celebrated primarily by Innocents and Mortar Board in announcing new members.

## Speech and Debate Team

Debate is considered the oldest student activity at Nebraska because of its association with literary societies, particularly Nebraska's first society, Palladian. Palladian met every Friday night and its "literary exercises" and debates were open to the public. Eventually Nebraska's literary societies pitted against those at other universities, such as the University of Kansas and Doane College in Crete, Nebraska. The first intercollegiate debate between Nebraska and Doane was held in 1882 and involved a chartered train from Lincoln to Crete, with accompaniment by the Cadet Band.

Today's speech and debate team, housed in the Department of Communication Studies, has won seven straight Big Ten tournament titles and has placed in the top ten at the national tournament for the past ten years. In 2018 a UNL team member brought home Nebraska's first National Championship in debate.

## The *Daily Nebraskan*

For decades, reading the *Daily Nebraskan* was part of many UNL students' daily routine. Now known as the *DN*, today's *Daily Nebraskan*—the University's only independent student newspaper—focuses on daily digital content and a monthly print magazine edition. Founded in 1871 as the *Monthly Hesperian Student*, the newspaper's most notable early leader was Willa Cather, who became managing editor in 1893 and stayed on until her graduation in 1895. The *Hesperian* changed its name in 1901 to the *Daily Nebraskan*.

Over the years the *Daily Nebraskan* has provided vocal leadership on a number of issues and controversies. In 1936 editor Jack Fischer worked to convince the Board of Regents to secure and spend Public Works Administration funds to build the Nebraska Union. In 1952 editor Ruth Raymond defended faculty accused of being communist sympathizers, and in the 1970s the paper covered UNL student protests. Online publication of the paper began in 1995, and most past editions are now archived online as part of an ambitious project to retain the *DN*'s history.

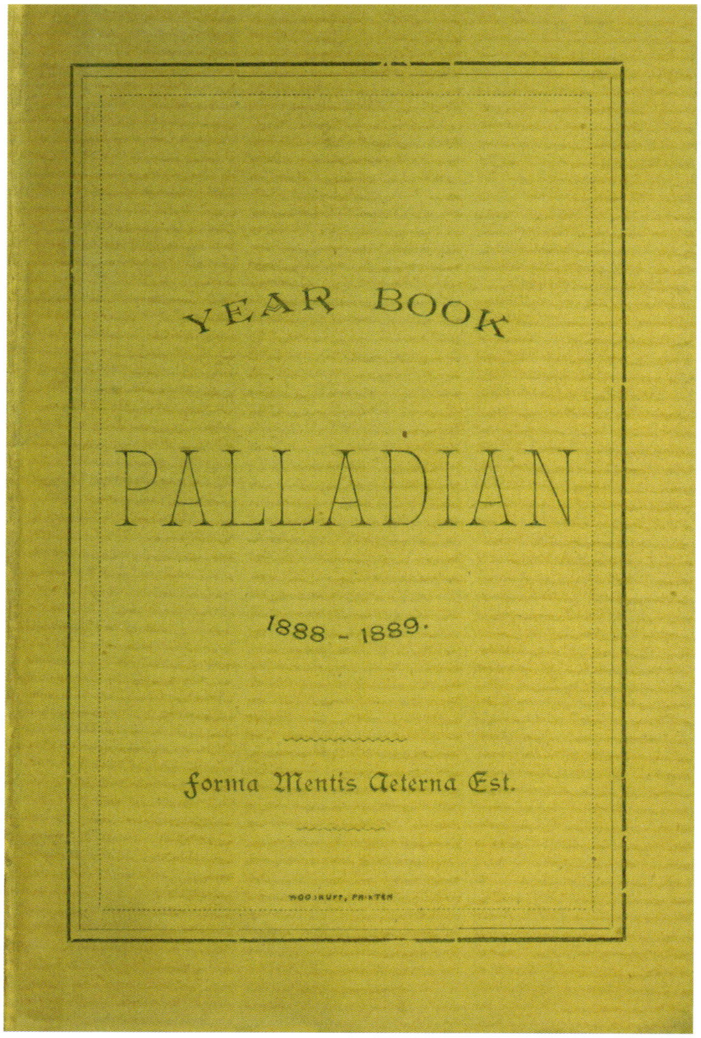


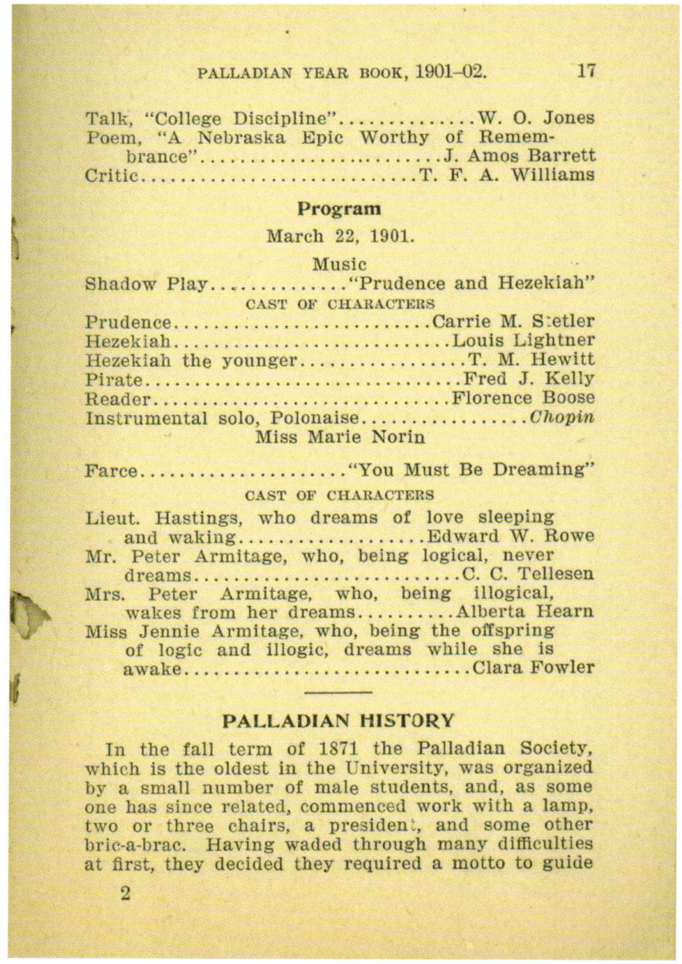
PALLADIAN YEAR BOOK, 1901–02. 17

Talk, "College Discipline"..............W. O. Jones
Poem, "A Nebraska Epic Worthy of Remembrance"..........................J. Amos Barrett
Critic...........................T. F. A. Williams

**Program**

March 22, 1901.

Music

Shadow Play..............."Prudence and Hezekiah"

CAST OF CHARACTERS

Prudence..........................Carrie M. Stetler
Hezekiah............................Louis Lightner
Hezekiah the younger.................T. M. Hewitt
Pirate................................Fred J. Kelly
Reader..............................Florence Boose
Instrumental solo, Polonaise.................*Chopin*
Miss Marie Norin

Farce....................."You Must Be Dreaming"

CAST OF CHARACTERS

Lieut. Hastings, who dreams of love sleeping and waking...................Edward W. Rowe
Mr. Peter Armitage, who, being logical, never dreams..........................C. C. Tellesen
Mrs. Peter Armitage, who, being illogical, wakes from her dreams..........Alberta Hearn
Miss Jennie Armitage, who, being the offspring of logic and illogic, dreams while she is awake............................Clara Fowler

**PALLADIAN HISTORY**

In the fall term of 1871 the Palladian Society, which is the oldest in the University, was organized by a small number of male students, and, as some one has since related, commenced work with a lamp, two or three chairs, a president, and some other bric-a-brac. Having waded through many difficulties at first, they decided they required a motto to guide

2

## Literary Societies

Like their counterparts at established eastern universities, Nebraska students established literary societies to augment the early pedagogy that was primarily memorization and recitation. Through their social activities, literary societies encouraged research, critical analysis, competition, and presentation skills. The first society, Palladian, was organized in 1871. Members consisted of men only (the first female members were inducted in 1875), so an all-female Pierian Literary Society formed in 1873, soon merging with the Adelphian Society. Two other societies, University Union and Delian, were established later. As the center of social life on campus, these societies met in University Hall, where weekly meetings involved programs of debate and oration, musical performance, and social activities. The chancellor, faculty, and the public often attended the spirited debates. Delian eventually merged with Union in 1931, and the combined organization folded completely in 1974. Palladian closed in 1969.

## Greek Life

Some 15 percent of Nebraska's undergraduate students are members of Greek-letter fraternities or sororities, producing campus leaders who consistently become engaged Nebraska alumni. Additionally, these chapters raise thousands of dollars for local and national philanthropies. In 2017 Nebraska launched Greek Vitality, an initiative focused on making Nebraska the best and most vibrant Greek community in the nation. Among its goals are enhancing students' value-based decision-making; empowering students to reach their potential and avoid high-risk behaviors; strengthening relationships between chapters, with others on campus, and with the larger community; and enhancing students' understanding of the consequences of their choices, rights, and responsibilities.

National fraternities came to Nebraska in the 1880s and immediately changed the student culture, which at the time revolved around literary societies. Phi Delta Theta, Sigma Chi, and Kappa Kappa Gamma were the first Greek-letter organizations; by 1900 eleven fraternities and five sororities were established on campus.

Worries that students were coming to the University for the social life of Greek houses rather than an education led the Board of Regents to demand the formation of an interfraternity council in 1905 and in 1906 the Intra-Sorority Council (now called the Panhellenic Association) to regulate Greek activities. Greek chapters boomed after World War II. In the 1960s and 1970s the civil rights movement made their lack of integration and racially restrictive policies more apparent, and most chapters began to realign priorities toward academics and philanthropy to remain relevant and vibrant. In addition to traditional Greek organizations, multicultural Greek organizations were originally formed to serve African-American and Latino/a students but have since expanded their reach to all minority students.

ΓΦΒ
GAMMA
ΓΦΒ

## Residence Halls

Nebraska's first students lived in rooms rented from Lincoln residents or in boardinghouses near campus until the 1930s, when cooperative halls for women opened under University supervision. The first women's residence complex, named after Carrie Belle Raymond, the director of music at the University, opened in 1932 and cost each resident $35 per month for full room and board. In 1938 Lincoln mayor Don Love provided money to expand the women's hall and later to build Love Cooperative Hall on East Campus.

In the 1940s, when more than 100 Nisei (second-generation Japanese-American) students matriculated at Nebraska, the issue of their housing caused controversy. The regents decreed that women's residence halls on 16th Street be restricted to whites only, but an international house was to be opened to female students of any race or color. Segregated men's residence halls were opened in 1945 and expanded in 1952; official "nondiscriminatory policies" were enacted in 1949. In 1954 Selleck Quadrangle residence hall opened.

To accommodate the growing number of baby boomers entering the University, two tower halls, Cather and Pound, opened in 1963, followed soon after by Abel and Sandoz Halls and Harper-Schramm-Smith later still. Cather and Pound were demolished in December 2017. By the early 2000s students' housing preferences had changed, and Nebraska embarked on a plan to build suite-style and apartment housing, including

Massengale Residential Center on East Campus and The Village on City Campus.

Nebraska now has fifteen residence halls—thirteen on City Campus and two on East Campus; total capacity is approximately 6,100 occupants. Most halls are not segregated by gender (though Love Hall houses women only). Many halls also host "learning communities," where students of like majors live together, take a shared class, and participate in activities as a group.

## Innocents Society / Mortar Board / Ivy Day

The chancellor's honor society, the Innocents, was organized in 1903 by then Dean of Law Roscoe Pound. Innocents started as an all-male society; women were invited beginning in 1976. The thirteen members of the group, selected as juniors, serve during their senior year and are chosen—based on leadership, character, and service—by the current group of Innocents. The society's signature look is a red robe, and the Innocents remain a uniquely Nebraska organization.

Black Masque, composed of thirteen women, was organized in 1905 as a female counterpart to Innocents. In 1921 this group affiliated with the national women's honor society Mortar Board and has remained the Black Masque chapter since. Chosen on the basis of scholarship and leadership, Mortar Board also emphasizes service to others, and membership is now open to men. In 1916 both societies began to announce their incoming classes on Ivy Day, which had started in 1901 as a spring festival held on the

first weekend in May. Ivy Day became an elaborate spring fete with a maypole dance, a queen with a court of honor, and other activities. The spring fair aspect of Ivy Day dwindled in the 1960s, but Innocents and Mortar Board still announce their new members on Ivy Day and recognize honorary members with a ceremonial planting of ivy on the lawns of Love Library.

## LGBTQA+ Advocacy

When Professor of English Lou Crompton team-taught homophile studies as an upper-division seminar in 1970, it was just the second time a course on the topic was taught at any public American university. The course had received academic approval from both the College of Arts and Sciences and the Graduate College, but the existence of the course agitated regents and legislators, who demanded it be withdrawn from the curriculum. University leadership declined.

Crompton and others were on the forefront of efforts to expand course offerings and opportunities for and about LGBTQA+ (Lesbian, Gay, Bi-/Pan-sexual, Transgender, Queer, Questioning, Asexual, Aromantic, Allies, plus additional identities relevant to sexual orientation, gender identities, and expression) individuals. Crompton was faculty advisor for the Gay Action Group, the first gay student organization at Nebraska (which organized in 1971), and later advised its successor, the Gay/Lesbian Student Association.

An ad hoc, independent Homophobia Awareness Committee, composed of faculty, staff, and students, formed to address issues such as: inclusion and representation in curriculum and University committees; language; homophobia awareness; safety; and domestic partner rights. Eventually the committee's name was changed to Committee on LGBT Concerns, now Pride@Nebraska. The LGBTQA+ Resource Center opened in 2007, and the campus continues to support its mission "to help build and sustain a socially just campus community that is welcoming and inclusive of all people of all sexual orientations, gender identities, and expression."

## Reserve Officers' Training Corps (ROTC)

The Morrill Act required all land grant institutions to offer military science, and Nebraska's first course was offered in 1876. About half the eligible male students enrolled, but the regents soon made the course mandatory. The arrival in 1891 of Lt. John J. Pershing as the University's military instructor elevated the program in stature and proficiency. In 1894 Pershing established a select drill unit, the Varsity Rifles, which was subsequently renamed Pershing Rifles when Pershing left Nebraska in 1895. The oldest continuously operating college organization devoted to military drill, the Pershing Rifles has chapters nationwide. Nebraska's chapter, dormant for more than a dozen years, was resurrected in 2017.

ROTC began in Nebraska in 1916. When the United States entered World War I the unit was converted into a Student Army Training Corps unit, which trained over 1,700 cadets. ROTC was reestablished in December 1918. The compulsory training program continued to grow, and by 1941, prior to U.S. entry into World War II, the University's cadets numbered 2,300. In 1945 a naval ROTC program was added to the curriculum, followed a year later by an air force unit.

All military science programs, voluntary since 1964, are administered under a joint ROTC curriculum committee, which was first organized in 1971. Currently, students from other colleges in the state—Doane College in Crete, Concordia University in Seward, Nebraska Wesleyan University in Lincoln, and York College in York—as well as students from the University of Nebraska at Kearney participate in Nebraska's ROTC program. Recently Nebraska ROTC, in partnership with the University of Nebraska Medical Center College of Nursing, achieved status as a U.S. Army Nursing Center of Excellence.

## Nebraska Student Veterans Organization

In 2007 a retired navy captain founded the Nebraska Student Veterans Organization (SVO). The SVO helps veterans transition from military duty to student life by providing academic and social support for veterans and their families. Peer mentoring assists veterans in navigating college life, finding resources both on and off campus, and helping veterans achieve academic and personal success. In 2017 *Military Times* magazine ranked Nebraska in the top twenty-five of "Best for Vets" colleges. That same year the journal *Military Advanced Education and Transition* named Nebraska a "top school" for following best practices in veterans' education. Approximately 2 percent of Nebraska's undergraduate students are veterans.

## Sem. Bot.

Among the most hallowed of Nebraska's early academic societies was Botanical Seminar, or Sem. Bot. Organized in 1886 with the help of then chancellor Charles Bessey (himself a botanist), Sem. Bot. was a serious effort to promote rigorous scientific study and research. Although seven men were listed as charter members, just five were regulars, including founder Roscoe Pound. (Excluded from membership, women organized their own Fem. Sem. Bot., although Sem. Bot was opened to women by 1898.) Sem. Bot. held weekly meetings in which members read, discussed, and critiqued scientific papers. While this seems dry and professorial now, Sem. Bot. was well known for its humorous take on topics, including writing satirical songs on botanical themes.

Sem. Bot. members successfully urged faculty to expand into other fields, notably animal disease, entomology, ornithology, parasitology, and bacteriology, and they undertook a botanical survey of Nebraska. Both Sem. Bot. and Fem. Sem. Bot. helped cement the importance of scholarly and scientific research at Nebraska. Following Charles Bessey's death in 1915, Sem. Bot. became more of a social society than a community of scholars, and by 1936 it had ceased to exist.

## Campus Recreation

Campus Recreation facilities and activities are an important part of student life, promoting wellness, leadership development, and social interaction. Over 750,000 check-ins are logged annually at Campus Rec facilities across the campuses. The department also manages over 175 acres of outside/green recreation space and administers the intramural and extramural sports, fitness, and wellness programs, as well as the sport clubs, recreation and leisure classes, academic recreational activity classes, outdoor adventure trips, aquatics, injury prevention and care, massage therapy, the climbing wall, the challenge course, the bike shop, gear and equipment rental, personal training, and youth activity programs. A new Recreation and Wellness Center opened on East Campus in July 2015, following two years of renovation to the historic East Campus Activities Building.

## International and Global Studies

Global Studies has three meanings at Nebraska: recruiting to Lincoln the University's more than 3,300 international students who come from over 130 countries, helping to ensure their academic and social success; supporting curriculums that present international perspectives and expose students to world cultures and experiences; and helping U.S. students who study abroad to gain firsthand real-world knowledge of global issues and people. Every year nearly 1,000 Nebraska students participate in Study Abroad opportunities. Some of these are short trips led by Nebraska faculty; others are semester-long opportunities at non-U.S. institutions in another country. Nebraska students have studied in fifty-six foreign countries in the past five years. The College of Business has a particularly robust global immersion program, which includes long-standing Study Abroad opportunities in England and Japan.

## Student Activism

From a full-fledged riot in 1948 over a lack of campus parking, to protests over sometimes questionable suspensions or firings of faculty members, to rallies against anti-communist policies, student activism is a dynamic part of campus life. The social and political unrest that spread across the nation during the 1960s also reached Nebraska's campus. By 1967 a campus "Student Bill of Rights" was endorsed by 7,000 Nebraska students in an all-campus vote, and students continued to advocate for change—both on campus, in the form of more flexibility in coursework and increased student control of social regulations, and off, including a 1969 march from campus to the State Capitol to protest U.S. involvement in the Vietnam War. In 1969 members of the Afro-American Collegiate Society organized a series of demonstrations to highlight the concerns of African-American students on campus. The society issued a list of twelve demands, including the founding of a black studies program.

The Kent State University shootings on May 2, 1970, which left four students dead, spurred rallies, protests, and strikes at colleges across the nation. At Nebraska, students—at one point as many as 2,000 of them—and several faculty members occupied the Military and Naval Science Building for a night. Negotiations led to an all-campus town hall, and nearly one-third of the student body voted to join striking campuses across the country. Most classes were held as normal, however, and the strike ended the following week.

Contemporary students continue to press for student rights, the protection of free speech, and the right to assemble while providing a safe and welcoming space for all.

## UCARE

Undergraduate Creative Activities and Research Experience (UCARE) is a unique-to-Nebraska program for undergraduate students to obtain paid opportunities to work with faculty in deep and enriching learning experiences. Students gain in-depth knowledge in their disciplines, learn research techniques, collaborate with faculty and peers, and present their findings at an annual research fair. Students in all disciplines are eligible for the program, and research projects have ranged from studying switchgrass plants grown for biofuel to identifying and cataloging the poems of Walt Whitman, and from exploring the effects of background noise on productivity to creating textiles made of corn. The UCARE program is supported by generous gifts from a Pepsi Quasi Endowment and Union Bank & Trust of Nebraska.

"Is that at right angles?" questions T. T. Aakhus of Takaro Nakae in a drawing class.

Pharmacy College

A. Artman E. Holscher R. Iler E. Kimura R. Mangold

Engineering Sophomores

## Nisei Students

Nebraska enrolled more than 100 Nisei students (second-generation Japanese Americans) during World War II, at a time when 120,000 people of Japanese descent were removed from the West Coast and incarcerated in internment camps following the December 7, 1941, attack on Pearl Harbor in Hawaii and the subsequent U.S. declaration of war on Japan.

Nearly 4,000 Japanes-American students already enrolled in West Coast colleges were expelled when the United States forcibly removed people of Japanese descent from those states. The National Japanese American Student Relocation Council worked to find academic homes for these displaced students. Nebraska accepted more than 100 students between 1942 and 1945, the third-most of any institution. Most students reported their Nebraska experience as welcoming, although some unkind behaviors were directed toward them. Nisei students who graduated from Nebraska became medical doctors, engineers, college professors, teachers, journalists, and one member of the U.S. Congress. In the 1990s Nebraska's Nisei alumni held an on-campus reunion, during which they endowed several scholarships and dedicated a Nisei Plaza near Kimball Recital Hall in gratitude for Nebraska's generosity.

## Student Government

While a student council had existed at Nebraska since 1917, in fall 1964 a "constitutional convention" was launched to reform student government, recommending that the Association of Students of the University of Nebraska (ASUN) be the "supreme" student governing body for facilitating relationships between students and faculty and administration.

On February 15, 1965, the ASUN name was officially chosen and after some wrangling with the academic senate over issues related to the student court, the official constitution was declared complete on March 12. Its basic principles laid out a three-part student government comprised of a directly elected leadership, a senate, and a judicial board. All students are automatically members of ASUN and are represented by elected senators. Students overwhelmingly voted to approve ASUN in March 1965. Student Council elections chairman Bob Kerrey (who went on to become a U.S. Medal of Honor recipient, the governor of Nebraska, and a U.S. senator from Nebraska) declared the elections successful with "a much better turnout than expected." ASUN began formally operating in the fall of 1966. In addition to being a voice for UNL students, ASUN sponsors numerous social events throughout the year and works to connect the University with the community.

## Rodeo Club

The University of Nebraska Rodeo Association (UNRA), a recognized student organization at UNL, has hosted an annual rodeo for nearly sixty years. UNRA is a member of the Great Plains Region of the National Intercollegiate Rodeo Association. About 250 contestants from six states compete in ten rodeos throughout the year to qualify for the College National Finals Rodeo held annually in Casper, Wyoming. The UNL Rodeo takes place each year during CASNR Week, a celebration of the College of Agricultural Sciences and Natural Resources. CASNR Week is planned, organized, and executed solely by students.

EADING 329

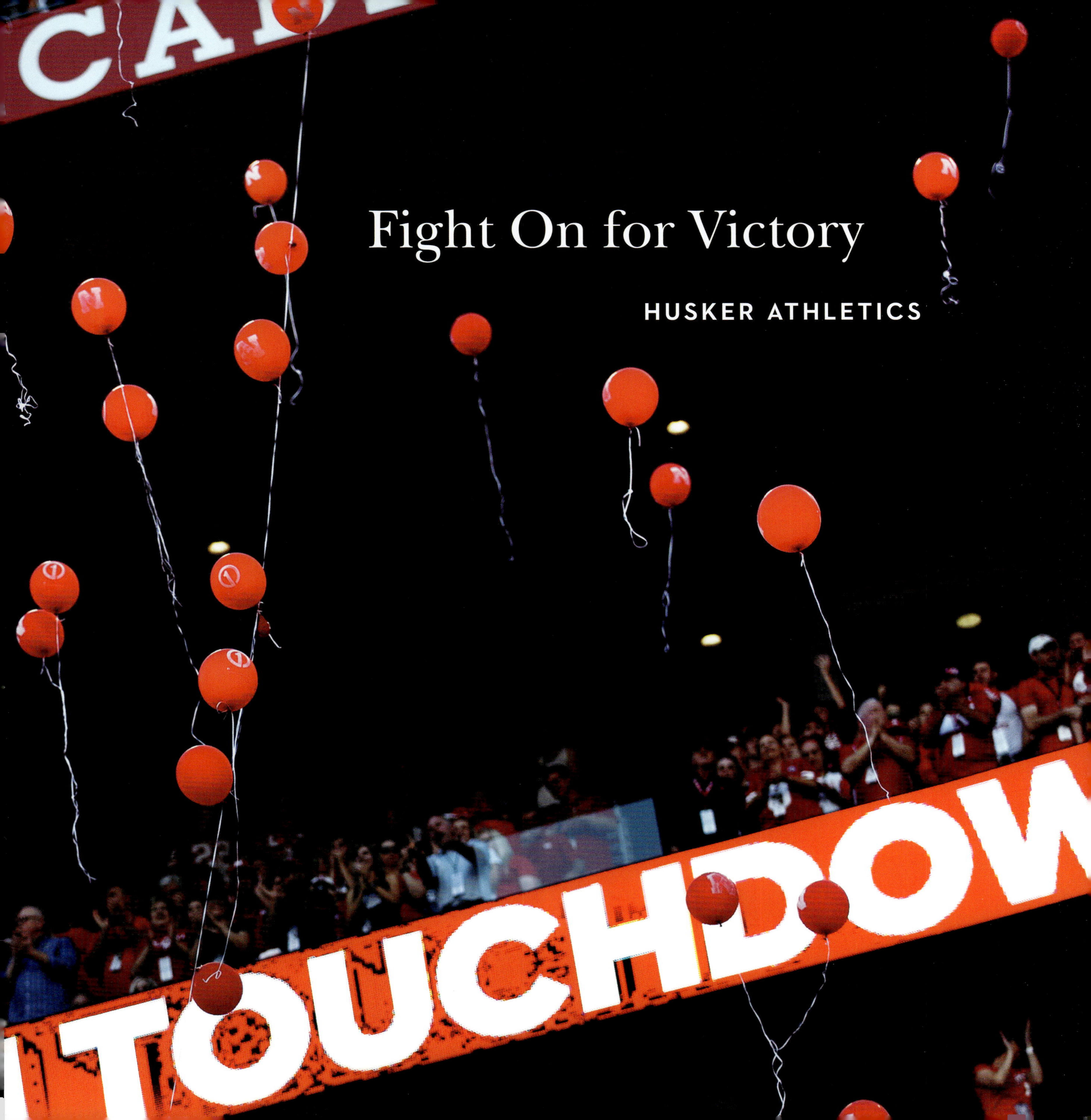

# Fight On for Victory

## HUSKER ATHLETICS

MEMORIAL STADIUM
N
N
OT THE GOAL BUT THE GAME: IN THE DEED T

NOT THE VICTORY BUT THE ACTION

NOT THE GOAL BUT THE GAME

IN THE DEED THE GLORY

Hartley Burr Alexander's stirring prose was originally carved on the southwest turret of Memorial Stadium prior to its opening in 1924; it now is inscribed across the exterior of the stadium's western face. Alexander's words describe fans' feelings for Nebraska athletics. Like fans everywhere, Huskers love to win; losing stings. But for many, the idea of the game, well and fairly played, is at the heart of what it means to be a Husker.

The University's interest in sports started early—the first recorded contest was a baseball game between the "University Nine" and the Yankee Hill Base Ball Club in October 1871. Nebraska won 46–11. Student pleas for a gymnasium prompted the 1879 opening of an exercise room in University Hall's basement, and in 1884 a room on the fourth floor was dedicated to women's calisthenics.

The University Athletic Association was launched in 1882 in an attempt to formally organize teams for competition in football, baseball, and tennis, and in fall 1889 the first football game was played at Nebraska—between the senior and sophomore classes. In 1891 Chancellor James Canfield allowed the University of Nebraska to begin competing in intercollegiate football.

Football became a symbol and point of pride for Nebraska. In 1962 the modern Big Red phenomenon began with the hiring of Bob Devaney as head football coach. Since then Nebraska has won five national championships in football and a total of twenty-six team NCAA national championships in five sports, including in men's gymnastics (eight), women's volleyball (five), women's bowling (five), and women's indoor track and field (three).

Women played team sports during the early history of the University, but intercollegiate athletics were dropped in the 1920s due to concerns that athletics were "unladylike" or "dangerous to women's bodies." The passage of the federal Title IX law in 1972 launched women's varsity sports at Nebraska. Nebraska currently fields twenty-two varsity teams and

competes in the Big Ten Conference, which it joined in 2011. Nebraska is proud to boast a nation-leading total of 333 CoSIDA/Capital One Academic All-Americans (as of July 1, 2018).

In 2013 a 50,000-square-foot expansion of Nebraska's East Memorial Stadium brought together athletic and academic researchers under one roof to study human behavior and performance. The Nebraska Athletic Performance Laboratory's multimethod, multidisciplinary approach improves performance and health for all Husker athletes through technology and academic expertise. The partnership is believed to be the nation's only joint on-campus athletic and academic research facility, a testament to Nebraska's commitment to student-athletes' performance, safety, and long-term health and well-being.

The Big Red phenomenon reaches far beyond the edges of campus, with members of Husker Nation found in locations spread across the globe. Husker athletes continue to reach new levels of success, making all of us proud to say Go Big Red.

SEARS
SEARS
SEARS
NCAA
NCAA
NCAA
NCAA
NCAA
2004
NATIONAL
COLLEGIATE
2006
DIVISION I
WOMEN'S
2015
NATIONAL
COLLEGIATE
BOWLING
CHAMPIONSHIP
2015
DIVISION
VOLLEYBALL
CHAMPIONSHIP
2001
INTERCOLLEGIATE
BOWLING
CHAMPIONSHIP
NATIONAL
CHAMPION
TEAM
1999
INTERCOLLEGIATE
BOWLING
CHAMPIONSHIP
NATIONAL
CHAMPION
TEAM
NATIONAL CHAMPION
SEARS
1993-1994

INDIANA
ILLINOIS
MICHIGAN STATE
UNIVERSITY
NEBRASKA
PURDUE
MICHIGAN
WISCONSIN
BADGERS

## Big Ten Conference

The oldest of the major athletic conferences, the Big Ten traces its lineage to 1895. Nebraska officially joined the conference in July 2011, becoming the twelfth member, and the conference has since grown to include two additional schools. More than 120 years after its inception, the Big Ten remains a national leader in both academics and intercollegiate athletics, producing billions in funded research and managing dozens of sports tournaments and championships. Big Ten programs have combined to win more than 450 team and 1,800 individual national championships, consistently taking home individual honors for athletic and academic accomplishments and fulfilling the Big Ten's mission of academic achievement and athletic success.

NEBRASKA
HUSKERS

## Memorial Stadium

Built to honor the Nebraskans who died in World War I and those who served in the Civil War and the Spanish American War, and funded by donations from across the state, Memorial Stadium was constructed in a mere ninety days and officially dedicated on October 20, 1923, during homecoming festivities. The stadium hosted its first game, a shutout rout of the Oklahoma Sooners, on October 13, and the team played the Kansas Jayhawks, the game ending in a scoreless tie, on dedication Saturday.

Originally open on both the north and south ends, frequent additions and renovations have enclosed the bowl and obscured the original facade. Current capacity is approximately 90,000, an impressive increase from the 1923 capacity of 31,000. The stadium has been sold out for every game since 1962, an ongoing NCAA record.

Memorial Stadium was the first college stadium to feature big screen televisions (installed in 1994) and artificial FieldTurf (laid in 1999). The most recent addition added 6,000 seats and an academic-athletic research facility housing the Center for Brain, Biology and Behavior.

First National Bank
FOOTBALL

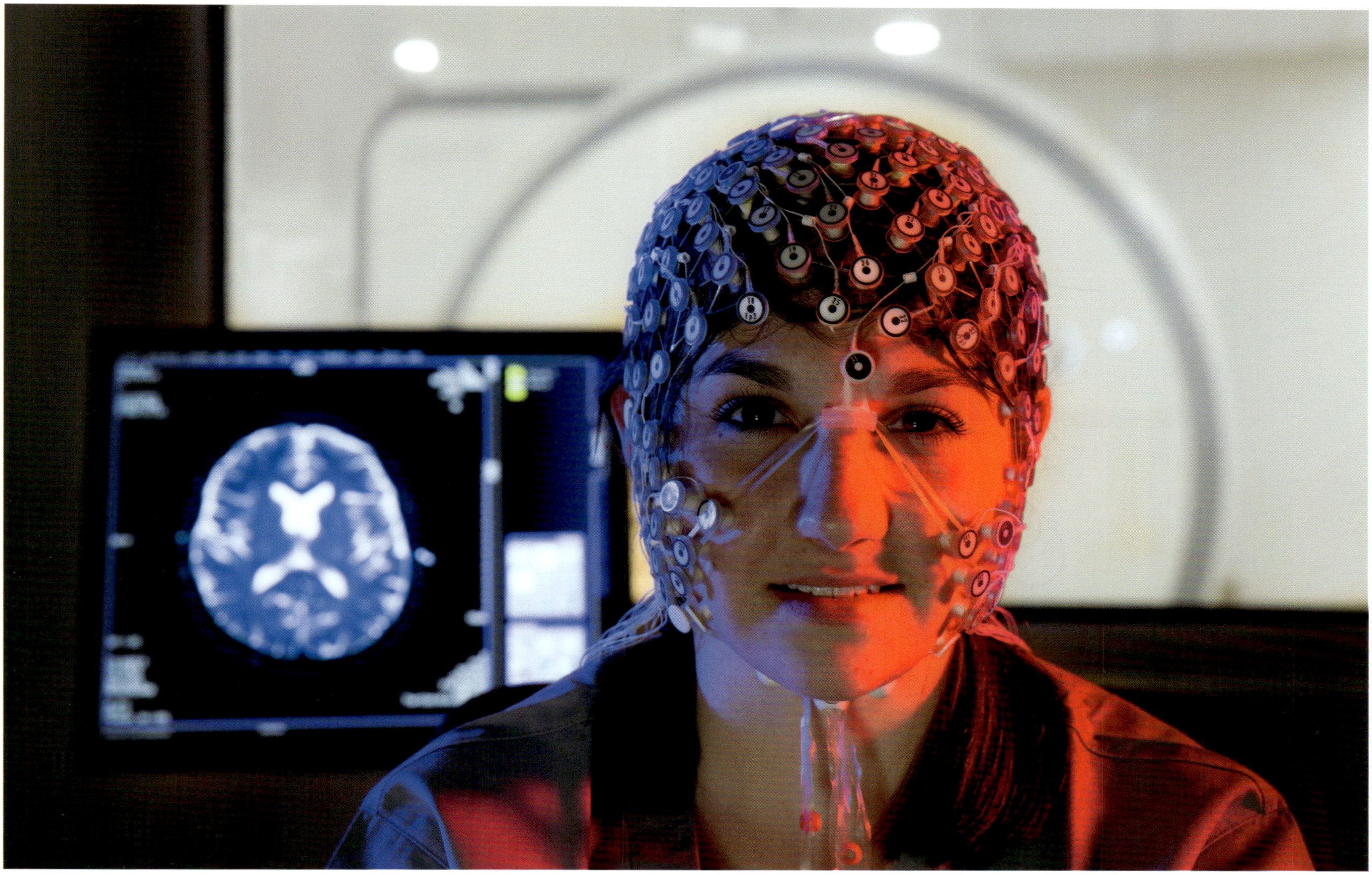

## Center for Brain, Biology and Behavior

Few world-class research facilities are located inside a football stadium, but from its offices in Nebraska's Memorial Stadium complex, the Center for Brain, Biology and Behavior, or CB3, brings together researchers in social, biological, and behavioral sciences and engineering to study brain function and its effects on human behavior. Scientists working in the state-of-the-art interdisciplinary research center, established in 2013, represent the academic spectrum, from neuropsychology and early childhood development to sensorimotor function and political science.

The center's functional magnetic resonance imaging capability (fMRI) records brain electrical activity and tracks eye movement. This combination of brain imaging and cognitive assessment equipment could lead to discoveries about brain function, head injury, human performance, and psychology that benefit athletes, the healthcare community, and broader society. One psychology research group within the center is using saliva to learn how biology affects behavior. The Salivary Bioscience Laboratory offers researchers a critical tool for investigating the biological components of disciplines like psychology, education, political science, criminology, and sociology.

## Husker Football

There is no doubt that football is the University's most recognized sports team, with a devoted fan base and success both on and off the field. Nebraska is one of only ten NCAA Division 1-A football teams to win eight hundred or more games, and the Huskers boast more victories against Power Five opponents than any other program, as well as the third-most victories of all time, behind only the University of Michigan and the University of Texas. Nebraska also has the most wins and the highest winning percentage of any program over the last fifty years, winning forty-six conference championships and five national championships (in 1970, 1971, 1994, 1995, and 1997). Nebraska claims three Heisman Trophy winners (Johnny Rodgers, 1972; Mike Rozier, 1983; Eric Crouch, 2001), sixteen players and nine coaches inducted into the College Football Hall of Fame, 108 Academic All-Americans, and over three hundred players going on to play in the National Football League.

Nebraska's football dynasty began with coach Bob Devaney, whose 1971 team is the only championship football team to beat the second-, third-, and fourth-ranked teams in the same season. Many Nebraskans can still recall the "Game of the Century" on Thanksgiving Day 1971, a 35–31 victory over No. 2 Oklahoma. Tom Osborne continued Nebraska's winning tradition with three national championships, including the 1995 team, considered the greatest college football team of all time. In 2018 former Nebraska quarterback Scott Frost returned to his home state to take the reins as head coach. A starter for Nebraska in 1996 and 1997, Frost played in the NFL until 2003, before turning to a coaching career.

Fans anxiously await the beginning of each new season, eager to welcome the pageantry of game day and cheer their team to victory, carrying on the Nebraska tradition of excellence.

## Herbie Husker and Lil' Red

Mascots Herbie Husker and Lil' Red are sideline icons known as much for their looks as their antics. Herbie, who debuted in 1974, originally wore denim overalls with an ear of corn poking out of his pocket and a cowboy hat emblazoned with a red "N." Over the years Herbie has been refined and buffed up from his original "farm boy" cartoon look to a more powerful and muscular character, still in denim and work boots but with more of an edge. Herbie was named the 2005 National Mascot of the Year.

Measuring eight feet tall and with the ability to bounce on his head, the Lil' Red balloon character appeared in 1993. Designed as a four-year-old kid in red overalls with a red "N" baseball cap worn sideways, Lil' Red's antics include dancing, collapsing his head and nose, spinning, and fast-shuffling. The Lil' Red operator wears a battery-powered air circulation system that brings in over 100 cubic feet of fresh outside air per minute, keeping Lil' Red inflated. Lil' Red won the NCAA National Mascot Competition in 1999 and was inducted into the Mascot Hall of Fame in 2007.

LIL' RED
SPORTS NIGHTLY MONDAY
1995
1992
1991
1988
1984

VOLLEYBALL CHAMPIONSHIP
Nebraska
26
Nebraska
3
NCAA
14

## Husker Volleyball

Founded in 1975, intercollegiate volleyball was the first women's sports team to compete for Husker Athletics. Since then the team has excelled, winning five national championships—in 1995, 2000, 2006, 2015, and 2017—and accumulating more wins than any other college volleyball program. Nebraska volleyball alumni include winners of the NCAA National Player of the Year, U.S. Olympians, all-conference players, thirty-eight Academic All-Americans, and four AVCA National Player of the Year (Allison Weston, 1995; Greichaly Cepero, 2000; Christina Houghtelling, 2005; Sarah Pavan, 2006). Incredible fan support enabled the program to move to the completely refurbished and rededicated facility at the Bob Devaney Sports Center in 2013. The Huskers have led NCAA volleyball in attendance every year since moving to the Devaney Center, with an average match attendance of 8,206. Husker volleyball holds the NCAA record for the most consecutive sellouts in any women's sport.

## Bob Devaney Sports Center

Bob Devaney Sports Center opened in 1976 as home to Nebraska's basketball programs, which used the building for thirty-seven years before moving to Pinnacle Bank Arena in 2013. The Devaney Center has also been home to Husker gymnastics, indoor track, wrestling, and swimming and diving. The center is named for longtime athletic director and football coach Bob Devaney. Built on then Nebraska State Fairgrounds land, the off-campus location was controversial in its day, as was the method of financing the building through a tax on cigarette sales.

The Devaney Center has been extensively renovated and upgraded over the years. The most recent overhaul occurred in 2013, when the main arena was repurposed for a state-of-the-art volleyball court and stadium. Bill and Ruth Scott, UNL graduates and generous supporters of the University, provided the lead gift for the project. The addition of the Hendricks Training Complex in 2011 opened additional facilities for student-athletes.

B1G
B1G
NEBRASKA

## Spirit Squad

The Husker Spirit Squad consists of the Cheer Squad, the Scarlets Dance Team, and mascots Herbie Husker and Lil' Red. Since 1903 more than 700 students have been members of the Yell Squad, Pom Squad, Coed Squad, and Cheer Squad. The Scarlets and Husker Cheer are all women, but the original cheer group was organized in 1903 by the then all-male Innocents Society, the chancellor's academic honor society. Two men composed the Cheer Squad until 1917, when three women joined. The Innocents Society voted in 1921 to end female participation, but women rejoined in 1944. In 1950 the squad again reverted to all men, but by the 1960s women returned to the sidelines. Men were on the team during the 1990s and early 2000s, but their participation ended when the squad discontinued lifts and tumbling. The current Cheer Squad has twenty-two members. The eighteen-member Scarlets Dance Team debuted in 1992. Both spirit groups are managed by professional members of Husker Athletics who are Nebraska Spirit Squad alumni.

## Cornhusker Marching Band

The Cornhusker Marching Band, billed as the "Pride of All Nebraska," got its start as an ROTC unit in 1879 to aid in military drills and marches. The original twelve-member band swelled to seventy-five men by World War I. Women were allowed to join the band briefly during World War II, due to the reduced number of available male students, but after the war ROTC pressed for a return to an all-male band. In 1955 the band split from the military program. Women joined the band in 1972 after Title IX was enacted.

As one of the top and best-known collegiate bands in the country, the Cornhusker Marching Band and its ensembles play before millions of people each year. The Cornhuskers are one of the few college bands to have performed at every major bowl game, beginning with the 1941 Rose Bowl. The current three-hundred-piece ensemble includes woodwinds, brass, percussion (battery and front ensemble), color guard, and twirlers. The Cornhusker Marching Band resides in the Glenn Korff School of Music, but three-fourths of its members are not music majors, instead representing over seventy academic majors from across the campus who play and march simply for the love of it.

## The Tunnel Walk

The Tunnel Walk at Memorial Stadium, which began in 1994, is now part of the football team's game day traditions. Each year a new and highly anticipated Tunnel Walk video is created incorporating sounds of Alan Parsons Project's "Sirius." Players leave the locker room after chanting the Husker Prayer, then touch a lucky horseshoe overhead and walk a red carpet to the gates on the northwest corner of the field. The stadium's Tunnel Walk gates are guarded by members of the Nebraska National Guard service units and opened by specially selected service men and women each game. After the team bursts through the gates, the Cornhusker Marching Band plays "Hail Varsity."

## Academic All-Americans

Nebraska athletes are just as dominant in the classroom, having won 333 CoSIDA/Capital One Academic All-America awards, more than any other school in the country. Three former Huskers are included in the Academic All-America Hall of Fame: Dave Rimington (football, class of 2004), Karen Jennings (women's basketball, class of 2008), and Pat Tyrance (football, class of 2009).

Academic All-Americans are honored with portraits displayed in the Dick and Peg Herman Family Student Life Complex, which is dedicated to innovative and comprehensive academic support for all Husker athletes. In addition to the staff who provide student support, the D. J. Sokol Enrichment Center, the Scott Technology Center, the Abbott Life Skills Center, the Papik Compliance Center, and the Lewis Training Table help ensure the success of all Nebraska student-athletes.

# Husker Legends

Nebraska has produced a bevy of award-winning coaches and athletes, each famous for individual accomplishments in his or her sport. Twelve stand out as true legends.

## BOB DEVANEY (1915–1997)

Bob Devaney led Nebraska's rise to athletic prominence. Devaney was affiliated with Nebraska for thirty-five years: as head football coach from 1962 to 1972, as athletic director from 1967 to 1993, and as athletic director emeritus from 1993 to 1996. He died in 1997 at age eighty-two. Devaney's record at Nebraska of 101-20-2 includes eight Big Eight titles, two national championships (1970, 1971), nine bowl appearances, two Outland Trophy winners, a Lombardi Award winner, and one Heisman Trophy winner. The football team's success under Devaney drove revenues that allowed Husker Athletics to grow into one of the few self-sustaining athletic departments in the NCAA.

## TOM OSBORNE (1937–PRESENT)

Bob Devaney's successor, Tom Osborne, continued Nebraska's tradition of athletic excellence. During Osborne's twenty-five-year tenure as head football coach, Nebraska won three national championships, including back-to-back titles in 1994 and 1995, and thirteen conference championships. His players also snared individual honors, including two Heisman Trophy, five Outland Trophy, and four Lombardi Award winners. Osborne's players also earned numerous Academic All-America honors and postgraduate scholarships and accolades. Osborne's record of 255-49-3 places him among the top college football coaches of all time.

After leaving the University, Osborne served as U.S. Representative from Nebraska's Third Congressional District from 2000 to 2006. In 2007 he returned to Nebraska, the school where he had earned master's and doctoral degrees, to head the Athletic Department. He undertook an impressive effort to upgrade facilities, including expansion of Memorial Stadium, construction of the Hendricks Training Complex and the Student Life Complex, and development of Pinnacle Bank Arena in Lincoln's Haymarket District. He also directed Nebraska's transition to the Big Ten Conference in 2011. Osborne retired in 2012.

Osborne was renowned for his coaching abilities and relationships with his players, even giving a eulogy at Brook Berringer's funeral. Berringer, a quarterback for Nebraska who started part of his junior season and helped lead the team to their 1994 and 1995 national championships, died in a plane crash in 1996. A statue of Osborne and Berringer standing side by side is installed outside Memorial Stadium. Osborne and his wife, Nancy, also founded the TeamMates Mentoring program to help students in elementary through high school succeed.

## TERRY PETTIT (1946–PRESENT)

Nebraska launched its women's volleyball program in 1975, and Terry Pettit took over as head coach in 1977. Under Pettit's watch Nebraska built a volleyball dynasty, winning twenty-one Big Eight and Big Twelve Championships and the NCAA national championship in 1995. Pettit retired in 1999 with an overall record of 694-148-12, including eighteen consecutive NCAA tournament appearances. He was named conference Coach of the Year nine times and national Coach of the Year twice. Many of his players won national accolades, including conference Player of the Year, National Player of the Year, and Academic All-America awards. Nebraska's success led to the popularity of volleyball as a sport in Nebraska high schools, creating a pipeline of eager and talented players who have contributed to the team's continuing success.

## JOHN COOK (1956–PRESENT)

John Cook succeeded Terry Pettit as Nebraska's head volleyball coach in 2000, taking over a team with a winning tradition and a passion to improve on near perfection. Cook has guided the Huskers to four national titles, nine Big Twelve titles, and three Big Ten championships, expanding the program's visibility and popularity throughout the state and the nation. Nebraska has produced numerous individual honors under Cook's watch, including nine U.S. National Team members, five U.S. Olympians, one Honda-Broderick Cup winner, two NCAA Top Ten Award winners, three Academic All-Americans of the Year, nineteen Academic All-Americans, one Big Ten Player of the Year, six Big Twelve Players of the Year, and three Big Twelve Co-Players of the Year. During Cook's tenure Husker volleyball players have combined for forty first-team All-Big Twelve awards and sixty-one Academic All-Big Twelve certificates, while since 2011 the Huskers have earned twenty-two All-Big Ten honors and forty-three Academic All-Big Ten accolades. Cook is a two-time AVCA National Coach of the Year (2000 and 2005) and is a seven-time conference Coach of the Year. He was inducted into the AVCA Hall of Fame in 2017.

## FRANCIS ALLEN (1943–PRESENT)

Francis Allen was affiliated with Nebraska for more than fifty years, first as a student-athlete, joining the gymnastics team in 1963, helping lead Nebraska to a Big Eight title in 1964. Allen became an assistant coach after graduating, then head coach in 1969. When Allen retired in 2009 he had served longer than any other Nebraska coach in any sport. Allen's teams won eight NCAA championships, with seven runner-up finishes and fourteen conference titles. Individually, Allen's athletes earned 172 All-America awards, forty-one individual event titles, and three Nissen-Emery Awards. Nine of his athletes represented the United States in the Olympics, and Allen coached the U.S. Olympics team in 1980 and 1992.

## JACK BEST (1845–1923)

Classes were canceled the afternoon of January 26, 1923, in observance of the funeral of beloved Nebraska athletic trainer Jack Best, following his death four days earlier at age seventy-seven. Best came to Nebraska in 1888 and served as an acting coach and trainer to every Cornhusker team beginning in 1890. Upon his death, the *Daily Nebraskan* reported Best had served "the last thirty-five years with loyalty and faithfulness that has made him famous and loved by every student and alumnus." Best was born and raised in England, where he boxed for a time under the name Jimmie Grimes. In the late 1880s he and his family moved to Nebraska, where he worked as a tanner before joining the University of Nebraska as a night watchman. He soon after became athletic trainer. Legend says that before the 1922 Thanksgiving Day football game, Best told the team it would be his last because he was dying. Nebraska defeated Notre Dame 14–6 that day, handing Notre Dame's Knute Rockne and his Four Horsemen the first of their only two defeats ever, both coming at the hands of Nebraska.

## GEORGE FLIPPIN (1868–1929)

George Flippin was Nebraska's first African-American student-athlete and only the fifth to play nationally at a predominantly white university. An all-around athlete, Flippin competed in wrestling, track and field, and baseball. Flippin won letters in football in 1892, 1893, and 1894 and was the star halfback for Nebraska's first victory against an out-of-state-opponent, when the Nebraska Bugeaters beat Illinois in 1892. That same year the University of Missouri forfeited a game to Nebraska because it refused to play against a black athlete. Flippin's parents were born slaves, and his father fought for the Union in the Civil War. Flippin was three when his mother died, and his father remarried a woman who was a piano student in Lincoln. Later his father and stepmother established a medical practice in Stromsburg, Nebraska. Flippin, too, became a medical doctor, also practicing in Stromsburg. He was the first African American inducted into the Nebraska Football Hall of Fame.

### INA GITTINGS (1885–1966)

A pioneer in women's athletics, Ina Gittings was born in Wilbur, Nebraska, and graduated from the University of Nebraska in 1906. She served as a physical education instructor at the University from 1906 to 1909 and director of the women's gymnasium from 1907 to 1916. Gittings was a star athlete at Nebraska who broke barriers throughout her career, most of which occurred after she left Nebraska for the University of Montana and later the University of Arizona. She also was a leader in the women's suffrage movement and served in the U.S. Army Medical Corps during World War I.

### MABEL LEE (1886–1985)

Mabel Lee was director of physical education for women at Nebraska from 1924 to 1952. A native Iowan, Lee inroduced basketball to her high school her sophomore year, and while at Nebraska she became nationally prominent in the field of physical education. She expanded physical education course offerings for women and increased women's participation in intramural sports from only 3 to 80 percent. While Lee advocated for women's sports, she was adamantly against intercollegiate women's competition, believing women should be active for health's sake only. Lee is memorialized on campus by Mabel Lee Hall, which has housed women's physical education courses and gymnasiums as part of the College of Education and Human Sciences.

### RHONDA REVELLE (1961–PRESENT)

Rhonda Revelle returned to her alma mater as head softball coach in 1993. She played for Nebraska from 1981 to 1983, helping lead the Huskers to the inaugural NCAA Women's College World Series in 1982. She owns nearly every Nebraska coaching record, winning more games than any other Nebraska coach, male or female. Revelle was inducted into the National Fastpitch Coaches Association Hall of Fame in 2010. She has been named Coach of the Year in three conferences—the Big Eight, the Big Twelve, and the Big Ten. Revelle is also known for coaching student-athletes who succeed off the field. Nebraska softball leads the nation with thirty Academic All-Americans, a total that is the third-highest in NCAA history among all female athletic programs. Revelle has helped college softball grow in popularity in the state and was instrumental in the development and opening of Bowlin Stadium in 2002.

## BILL STRAUB (1951–PRESENT)

In his twenty-six years at Nebraska, Bill Straub's bowling teams have won twelve national titles. His women's bowling teams have won five NCAA team championships and five Intercollegiate Bowling Championships (IBCs) (prior to NCAA's official sponsoring of bowling). Straub's team finished as the NCAA runner-up in 2017. Straub also coached two men's IBC championships. Since the NCAA first sponsored women's bowling in 2004, Nebraska is the only program to have qualified for the NCAA championship every season. Straub has coached seven bowlers who have won a combined nine Player of the Year awards. A prominent and successful bowler himself, Straub has won more honors and titles than any other Nebraska bowler. He has been named National Tenpin Coaches Association Coach of the Year three times.

## WILBUR S. WOOD (UNKNOWN)

A student-athlete at Nebraska from 1907 to 1910, Wilbur Wood was Nebraska's first African-American basketball player. He was the second African American to play college basketball at a predominantly white institution. After earning his degree in 1909, Wood took graduate courses in chemistry and pharmacy during his final basketball season; he coached Nebraska's freshman team from 1910 to 1911 and won Nebraska's fencing championship in 1910. Wood withdrew from Nebraska in 1911. It is believed he later operated a pharmacy in Kansas City.

Frontiers of Knowledge
RESEARCH AND CREATIVE ACTIVITY

Land grant universities are described as having a three-part mission: teaching and learning, research and discovery, and service and outreach. When Nebraska opened its doors in 1871, the teaching part was functioning, but the other parts were essentially nonexistent. The hiring of Charles Bessey in 1884 changed the equation. Bessey believed in a more hands-on approach to teaching, and he also deeply believed in "experimentation" and "science through practice." Bessey helped write the 1887 federal Hatch Act that enabled "experiment stations" at land grant universities and provided each state $15,000 in annual federal funding to support research. Soon after, Nebraska's legislature matched the funding.

This new focus on research as a way to inform learning had immediate benefits for Nebraska. Henry Baldwin Ward created the first lab course in the country to study parasitology; Harry K. Wolfe created the first lab course in psychology; Lawrence Bruner opened a lab in entomology; Bessey one in botany. Nebraska's graduate school, the first located west of the Mississippi, launched in 1896. Many of the students who graduated from the University during this era earned acclaim in their respective fields, including Willa Cather, Dorothy Canfield Fisher (inset, left), Roscoe Pound, Louise Pound, Frederic Clements, and George Sheldon.

Bessey's influence placed the University of Nebraska on a path to excellence in research. From that meager research budget of $30,000 in 1887, Nebraska now has an annual research expenditure budget of over $300 million. Nebraska has continued to excel in those early disciplines—plant science, physics, English, history—and currently leads research in energy sciences, human and animal virology, brain studies, early childhood education, lasers, international physics, computing, and transportation safety.

The link between University research and the state's economy has never been stronger. Nebraska leads world efforts to conserve water while improving crop yields to satisfy growing demands for food and water; an interdisciplinary focus on developing entrepreneurism has helped students launch start-ups and businesses across the state; the Buffet Early Childhood Institute is training early childhood professionals; and tens of thousands of graduates are employed in our state.

The research conducted in the University's classrooms and laboratories and the fieldwork undertaken across the globe have had a profound impact on countless aspects of our lives. The University of Nebraska will continue to be a leader in research initiatives, making new discoveries, training future researchers, and expanding knowledge.

## Robert B. Daugherty Water for Food Global Institute

The University of Nebraska has always been a leader in research on water, agriculture, and the management of critical natural resources. Recognizing these unique strengths, in 2010 NU president James B. Milliken, working with UNL chancellor Harvey Perlman and vice chancellor for research Prem Paul, led development of the Robert B. Daugherty Water for Food Global Institute, a research, education, and policy institute focused on global food and water security. A $50 million gift from the Robert B. Daugherty Charitable Foundation established the institute. Daugherty, the founder of the world's most successful irrigation company, Valmont Industries, was committed to the efficient and sustainable use of water to feed a growing world population.

The annual Water for Food Conference, which began in 2009, has attracted attendees from dozens of countries. The institute supports more than one hundred faculty fellows, global fellows, postdoctoral researchers, and students engaged in projects in seventy-seven countries, from using drones to measure drought stress and improve irrigation efficiency in Nebraska to working with partners in Brazil to sustainably increase irrigation.

More than eighty scientists affiliated with the institute are working to close water and agricultural productivity gaps,

improve groundwater management for agricultural production, enhance high-productivity irrigated agriculture, develop freshwater and agricultural ecosystems and public health, and manage the impact of drought on agriculture. Many of the projects involve using software and technology to help farmers, policymakers, scientists, and others make wise decisions about water use and distribution. Two UNL courses, including Water in Society, an undergraduate discovery class developed with funding from the National Science Foundation, and a graduate-level seminar are preparing future leaders and scientists to carry on the Water for Food mission.

## Wheat Breeding

In 1963 the University of Nebraska released a new hard red winter wheat variety called Scout. Scout became the top wheat variety in the United States for the subsequent ten years, being grown on more than 8 million acres or 25 percent of American wheat acreage. This was the beginning of Nebraska's dominance in wheat research and breeding, led by internationally known agronomists John W. Schmidt, Virgil Johnson, and their colleagues Rosalind Morris and Paul Mattern. In more than thirty years of active research, beginning in the early 1950s, this team developed and released twenty-eight new varieties of hard red winter wheat that was grown on 20 percent of U.S. acreage and in thirty-five other nations. P. Stephen Baenziger, who took over as UNL's wheat breeder when Schmidt retired in 1986, has continued Nebraska's tradition of excellence in cereal breeding, releasing forty varieties of wheat, barley, and triticale. The Nebraska wheat breeding team received a USDA grant in 2016 to develop higher-yielding lines of hybrid wheat that can meet the rising global demand for this staple crop, helping to maintain Nebraska's important role in agricultural research.

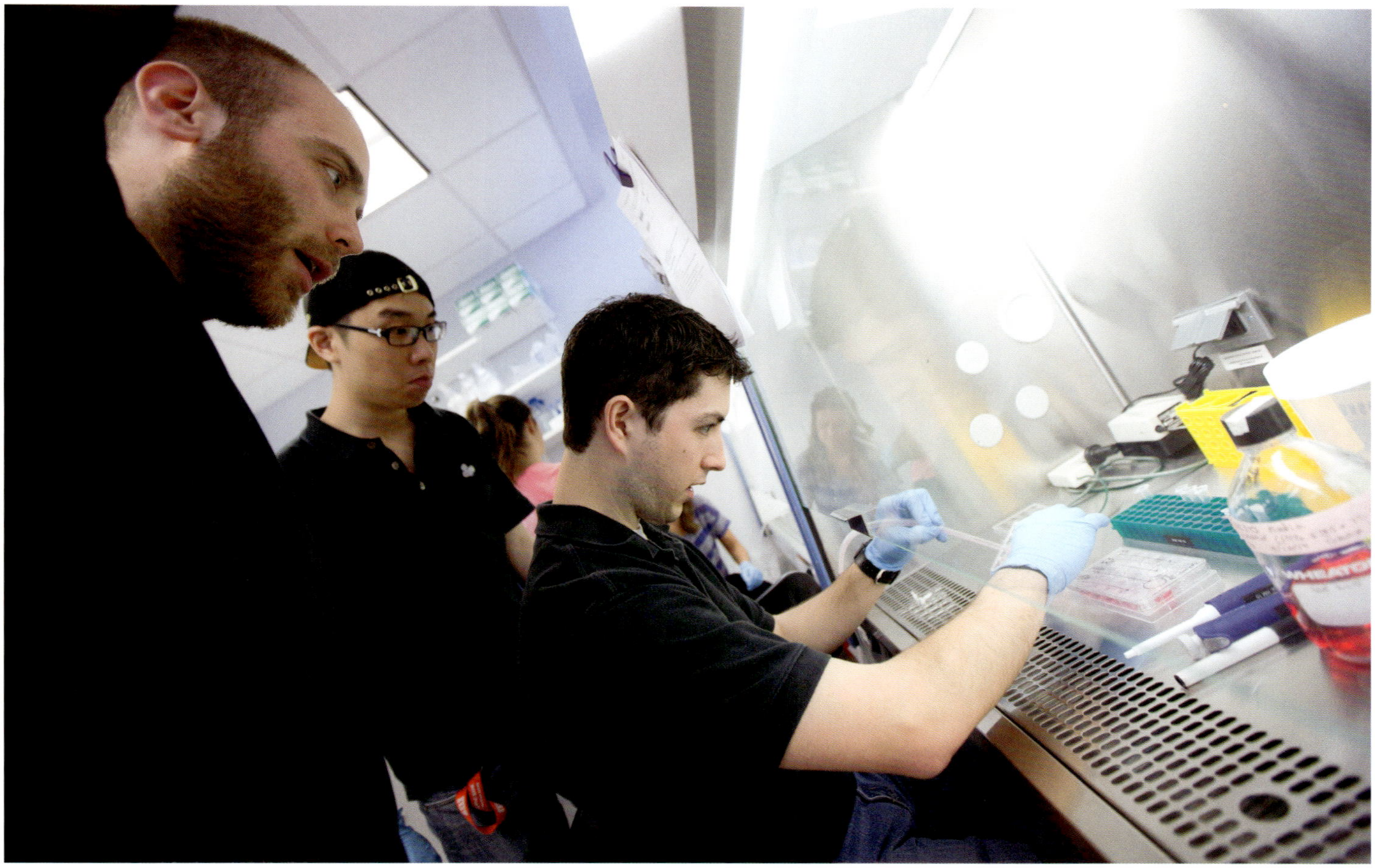

## National Strategic Research Institute

Founded in 2012, the National Strategic Research Institute (NSRI) at the University of Nebraska is the only University-affiliated research center in the country dedicated to delivering solutions for combating weapons of mass destruction (WMD) to U.S. Strategic Command (USSTRATCOM). NSRI provides research and development for the U.S. Department of Defense, the U.S. Department of Homeland Security, and other governmental agencies in multiple mission-critical competency areas—including development of medical countermeasures to WMD; nuclear detection and forensics; consequence management; chemical and biological weapons detection; and space, cyber, and telecom law.

In 2018 NSRI received a five-year, $92 million contract with the U.S. Air Force to expand research opportunities across the NU system to help meet the needs of USSTRATCOM and the Department of Defense. The contract will allow NSRI to maintain ongoing work, like improving a vaccine for the toxin ricin, advancing the performance of metals used on military vehicles, improving laser technology used to detect explosives, and developing new research projects by faculty, researchers, and students from across the University.

## Center for Digital Research in the Humanities

Nebraska is a leader in digital scholarship, thanks to a bit of risk-taking and decisions to prioritize emerging projects in the humanities. The gamble paid off in 2005 with the launch of the Center for Digital Research in the Humanities, now considered one of the nation's premiere centers of digital scholarship. The center thrives on collaboration and interdisciplinary work. Projects include the Willa Cather Archive and the Journals of the Lewis and Clark Expedition Online. The Walt Whitman Archive is an enormous ever-changing project that is collecting, digitizing, analyzing, and publishing all known works by American poet Walt Whitman. Like all digital scholarship, a key factor is that items can be continuously added, annotated, edited, and updated. The center also has several projects important to preserving the language and heritage of two Nebraska tribes—the Ponca and the Omaha; another was the digitization of emancipation documents of more than three thousand enslaved people who lived in Washington DC during the Civil War.

With more than forty projects underway involving dozens of scholars at Nebraska and other locations, the center also has undergraduate and graduate students engaged in research, offering a graduate certification and an undergraduate minor. The center has attracted more than $10 million in grant funding for various projects.

## Jeffrey S. Raikes School of Computer Science and Management

When the idea for the Jeffrey S. Raikes School of Computer Science and Management was conceived in 1999, the goal was to create world-class leaders and innovators in business and computer science. The school has achieved that and more. The premise: select high-ability undergraduate students to live, study, and work together over their four years on campus, with the final year's capstone coursework, called Design Studio, focused on working for actual companies or institutions.

The best example of this homegrown enterprise is Lincoln-based Hudl, a software company that uses technology to help coaches and athletes maximize on- and off-field performance. Founded by three Raikes School graduates in 2006, Hudl's tools allow coaches and athletes to use video to interact with statistics, create highlight reels, and develop methods to improve performance. Hudl has more than 4.3 million unique users worldwide and employs more than a thousand people in fifteen countries.

The Raikes School opened in the Esther Kauffman Academic Residence Center under the name J. D. Edwards Honors Program in Computer Science and Management. It was renamed for Jeffrey Raikes, a Nebraskan who until 2014 was CEO of the Bill and Melinda Gates Foundation.

## Center for Plant Science Innovation

Plant science research has been a cornerstone of Nebraska's research agenda since the University's founding. The Center for Plant Science Innovation, established in 2008, is part of Nebraska's Institute of Agriculture and Natural Resources and connects plant biology research between UNL's City and East Campuses. The center was created as an interdisciplinary research and development, training, and mentoring program focused on molecular plant sciences.

Nebraska is currently part of a fifteen-institution research project funded by the U.S. Department of Energy that is looking for ways to develop and use biomass products as a sustainable energy resource. The goal is to genetically enhance sorghum, a drought-tolerant plant able to grow on marginal land, to make sorghum more oil-rich and a possible substitute for use in petroleum products like plastics and jet fuel.

## Cather Project

Nebraska has been foundational to the establishment of Willa Cather as a central figure in American culture. The Cather Project, designated by the University as a Program of Excellence in 2002, is a specialist academic unit dedicated to research and teaching related to Cather. The Cather Project produces the Willa Cather Scholarly Edition, a project initiated by Professor Susan J. Rosowski in the 1980s and published by the University of Nebraska Press, which offers deeply annotated editions of Cather's novels and poetry. The Cather Project cosponsors the Willa Cather International Seminar, a biennial conference of Cather scholars and enthusiasts that provides a forum for new scholarship; papers from the conference are published in the series Cather Studies. The Cather Project also partners with University Libraries to acquire important Cather archival material, to bring top Cather scholars to UNL to present lectures, and to support new creative adaptations of Cather's work.

## Nebraska Food for Health Center

Nebraska's research strengths in agriculture, animal husbandry and plant breeding, biomedical sciences, and genetics come together in the Nebraska Food for Health Center, launched in 2016. The goal of the center is to improve the health and lives of people worldwide by developing hybrid crops and foods that improve the quality of life of those affected by critical diseases, including heart disease, diabetes, obesity, cancer, inflammatory bowel disease, and mental disorders.

The Raikes Foundation of Seattle, cofounded by Nebraska native Jeff Raikes and his wife, Tricia, committed a challenge grant to support the center. The Bill and Melinda Gates Foundation also made a gift to honor Jeff Raikes's service as the foundation's CEO. The center, housed at the Food Innovation Center, a state-of-the-art facility for food science research and public-private partnerships on Nebraska Innovation Campus, brings together faculty from the University of Nebraska Omaha, and from the University of Nebraska Medical Center, to tie gastrointestinal and biomedical research to agriculture, plant and animal breeding, and genetics. A major goal of the Food for Health Center is to develop foods with proven health benefits, particularly those that affect the human gut microbiome—the collection of all the beneficial and potentially harmful microorganisms in the human digestive system that can affect health and well-being. The center also prepares students for careers in food health, as researchers, food and health industry leaders, and food innovation entrepreneurs.

## Nebraska Bullying Prevention and Intervention Initiative

Led by Susan Swearer, Willa Cather professor of educational psychology, the Nebraska Bullying Prevention and Intervention Initiative looks at ways to reduce the incidence of bullying in schools. In 2011 Swearer and others who study bullying and peer victimization launched the Bullying Research Network, which has more than two hundred researcher members in eighteen countries. The network links researchers interested in peer-reviewed, data-based decision-making models for responding to and reducing bullying behaviors.

The Empowerment Initiative Lab, founded in 2013, facilitates research into the various individual, social, and societal factors that are needed to create supportive environments for children, youth, families, and schools. Swearer is chair of the research advisory board for the Born This Way Foundation, founded in 2012 by musician Lady Gaga to create a kinder, braver, and more positive world for youth.

## Czech Language Instruction

Some 93,000 Nebraskans, or 5.5 percent of the state's population, claim Czech heritage, the largest percentage of any state. The University of Nebraska has been a center of language and Czech heritage, one of the few in the United States. In 1904 a Komensky (Comenius) Club was organized at Nebraska, and in 1905 thirteen ethnic Czech students petitioned for a Czech language course. In 1907 the Department of Slavonic Languages and Literatures was organized; Willa Cather's iconic novel *O Pioneers!* was translated into Czech by the University after its publication in 1913. Antiwar sentiment caused the regents to terminate the Slavonic Department in 1920, but Chancellor Samuel Avery reinstated Czech language instruction that same year. In 1980 and 1993 budget woes threatened the program's survival, but the support of Nebraska's Czech community has kept the program flourishing. Nebraska's Komensky Club was honored by the Czech Republic in 2005 for its work in preserving the Czech culture in Nebraska, and the University now has student exchange programs with the Czech Republic.

The Cornhusker

Komensky Club

Kouba Faytingar Kastl C. Kuska Vavra
H. Kuska Kaspar Nikl Krejci Pospisil Svoboda Janovsky Vogeltanz
Zrust Krikac Sukovaty Hrbkova Svoboda Klepetko Hromas

## Omaha Language Instruction

Nebraska students and scholars have contributed to keeping the language spoken by Omaha Tribe members alive and thriving. The late Mark Joseph U'thixide Awakuni-Swetland (1956–2015), who joined the University in 2000, created a Native language program and assembled a team to design instructional materials for the Omaha language. In partnership with Omaha tribal leaders and researchers at Wayne State College and Nebraska, Awakuni-Swetland developed an Omaha-Ponca digital dictionary and other reference materials for the Omaha language. At the time of his death the associate professor of anthropology and ethnic studies was working on an Omaha language textbook, *The Omaha Language and the Omaha Way: An Introduction to Omaha Language and Culture*, published by the University of Nebraska Press in 2018.

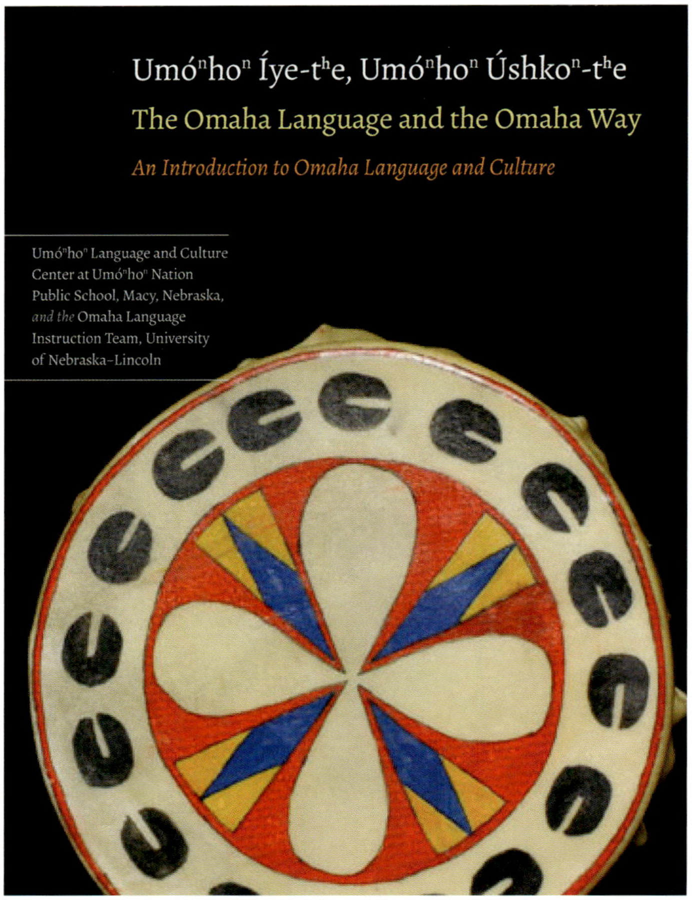

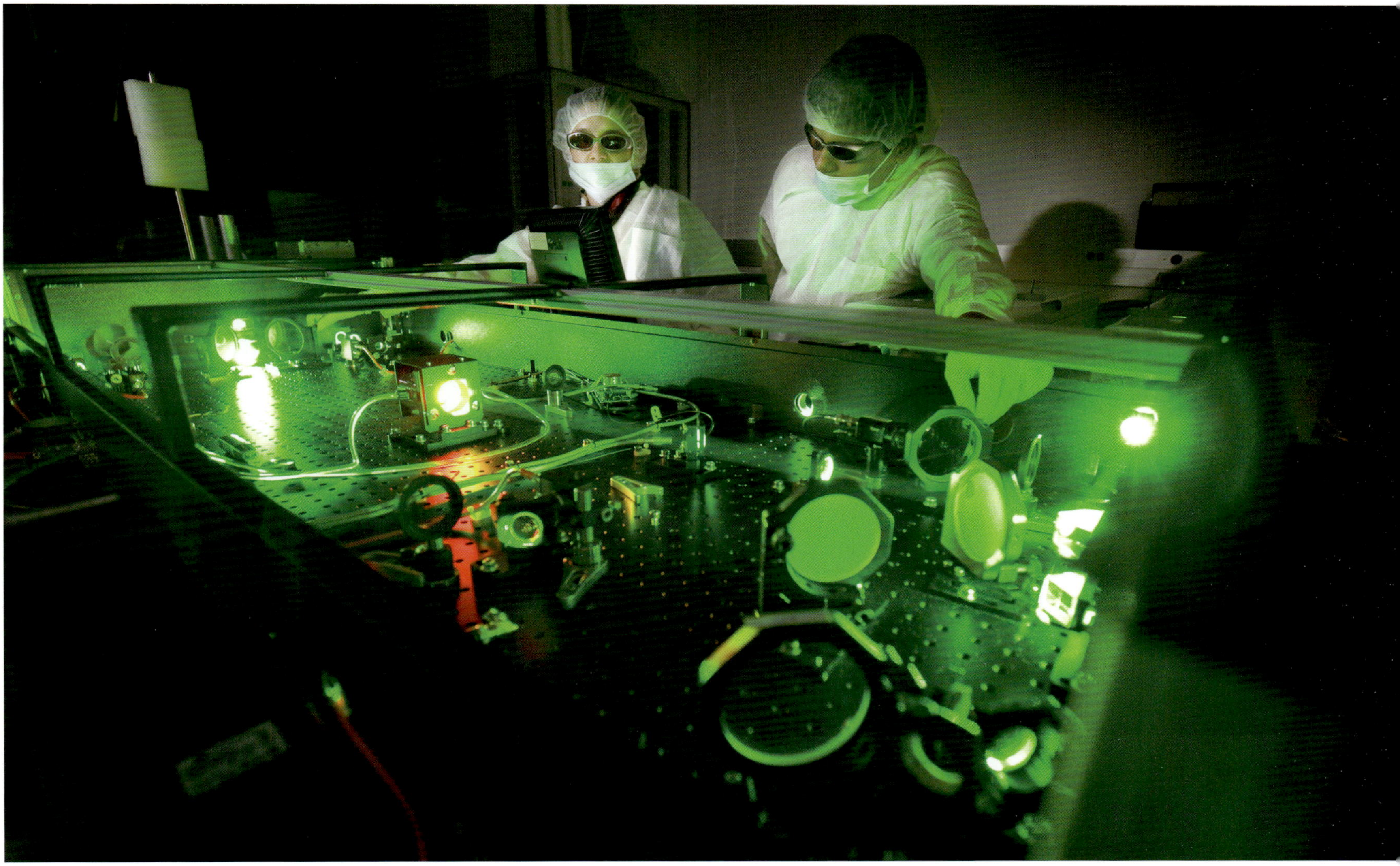

## Extreme Light Laboratory

When Nebraska physicists in 2017 focused laser light to a brightness one billion times greater than the surface of the sun—the brightest light ever produced on earth—they were building on a century of pioneering work in optics and nuclear and atomic physics at the University. DeWitt Bristol Brace came to Nebraska in 1887 and propelled the Physics Department to national prominence through his research into optics. Theodore "Ted" Jorgensen, who earned his bachelor's degree (1928) and master's degree (1930) from Nebraska, and a PhD in theoretical physics at Harvard (1935), returned to Nebraska in 1938 as a professor of physics. After working at Los Alamos National Laboratory during World War II, Jorgensen built a specialized underground, concrete-lined room on campus to house an ion accelerator for his experiments in nuclear and atomic physics. By mid-2006 Jorgensen's old lab had become the Extreme Light Laboratory and home to the Diocles laser. Diocles allows observation of changes in the interaction between light and matter, yielding a new type of X-ray with the potential to generate extremely high-resolution imagery for medical, engineering, scientific, and security purposes.

## NET Public Broadcasting

Nebraska Educational Telecommunications (NET) serves as Nebraska's Public Broadcasting Service (PBS) and network of National Public Radio (NPR) stations, connecting communities and celebrating Nebraska through educational services. The process of establishing NET began in 1951 when the Board of Regents petitioned the Federal Communications Commission for a noncommercial channel for educational use in Lincoln. The station first broadcasted on November 1, 1954, becoming only the ninth public station in the country. NET's founding director, Jack G. McBride, worked to establish a statewide network of public television stations with content originating from Lincoln. Many locally produced NET programs have aired on PBS, including *Reading Rainbow*, which NET co-developed and co-owned for more than two decades. NET also produces the longest-running show in public television, *Backyard Farmer*, which first aired in 1953.

Ron Hull joined NET in 1955 as the network's producer-director. Still active (after an official retirement in 2003), Hull is now senior advisor. Over the years Hull has interviewed numerous luminaries (such as Mari Sandoz, John Neihardt, Sandy Dennis, Dick Cavett, Eva Marie Saint, Vivian Vance, and Ken Burns), guided and produced programs, helped bring television to Vietnam, and advised PBS stations on how to create dynamic educational programming. In 2014 NET honored Hull by renaming its main studio after him.

In 1972 NET moved from the Temple Building on City Campus to its current location on East Campus. NET continues to engage learners of all ages and diverse communities in civil conversations and to celebrate Nebraska's cultural and creative achievements through exceptional content, educational services, community relationships, and advanced technologies.

## Nebraska Center for Virology

Viruses lie at the heart of many threats facing society: HIV/AIDS, hepatitis C, influenza, viral agents as bioweapons, food contaminants, and plant diseases that can ravage food production. Since the early twentieth century Nebraska has been at the forefront of virology research aimed at understanding and combatting these threats. In 1922 botanist George Peltier discovered wheat streak mosaic virus, a pest that still plagues wheat crops today. In the 1950s Myron Brakke pioneered virus purification techniques, eventually developing a specialized spinning rotor for the task. For this and other work Brakke was elected to the National Academy of Sciences in 1974, the first Nebraska faculty member to receive that honor. The 1970s brought more discoveries: Charles Mebus developed the first vaccine against rotaviruses and Anne Vidaver discovered the Cystovirus bacteriophage in 1973. James Van Etten discovered a new class of algae-infecting viruses in 1980 and was elected to the National Academy of Sciences in 2003.

This rich history in virology brought Charles Wood, an expert in molecular virology and the study of HIV, to UNL in 1996. Wood led development of the Nebraska Center for Virology (NCV), winning a $10.7 million National Institutes of Health Center for Biomedical Excellence grant in 2000 to establish the center. The center is housed in the Ken Morrison Life Sciences Research Center, named for the Hastings, Nebraska, businessman and UNL supporter who contributed the lead gift for the building's construction. With partners at the University of Nebraska Medical Center and Creighton University and Van Etten as its associate director, the center catalyzed an explosive growth in virology research in Nebraska. The NCV funds research projects for early career faculty and has trained scores of undergraduate, master's, and doctoral students, the next generation of virologists. That impact has reached beyond Nebraska. In Africa, Wood and his colleagues developed a twenty-year partnership with the University of Zambia Teaching Hospital in order to train health professionals in Zambia. In addition, Zambian students have trained at UNL then returned to their country to carry on the battle against HIV and AIDS-associated cancers.

UNIVERSITY OF NEBRASKA PRESS

## University of Nebraska Press

Founded in 1941, the University of Nebraska Press publishes scholarly and general interest books and journals under several imprints: Nebraska, Bison Books, and Potomac Books, and, by special arrangement, the Jewish Publication Society. In 2018 the press published 160 new books and had about 4,000 books on its backlist. The largest university press between Chicago and California, Nebraska also ranks as one of the largest in revenues of university presses nationally. In addition to books, the press also publishes thirty-one journals. The press primarily publishes in the areas of Native and indigenous studies, history, sports, literary fiction, fiction in translation, and creative nonfiction. Under its Potomac imprint the press publishes books on current, national, and military affairs. The press's bestselling title, *Black Elk Speaks* by John G. Neihardt, is approaching sales of one million copies.

## *Prairie Schooner*

Nebraska's award-winning literary magazine, *Prairie Schooner*, was founded by English professor Lowry Wimberly and first published in 1927. Over the years *Prairie Schooner* has published works by literary giants—Pulitzer Prize winners, Nobel laureates, U.S. Poet laureates, and MacArthur and Guggenheim fellows, including Truman Capote, Joyce Carol Oates, Mari Sandoz, Eudora Welty, and Tennessee Williams. The quarterly magazine is a collaboration of the University's Department of English and the University of Nebraska Press. Despite its name, which suggests a regional or Great Plains focus, the magazine publishes both American and international authors and is read worldwide. *Prairie Schooner* also publishes the Fusion digital series, which features collaborations between *Prairie Schooner* and online literary entities from around the world to create dynamic fusions in literature and art. In 2001 Nebraska alumna Glenna Luschei endowed *Prairie Schooner* in perpetuity.

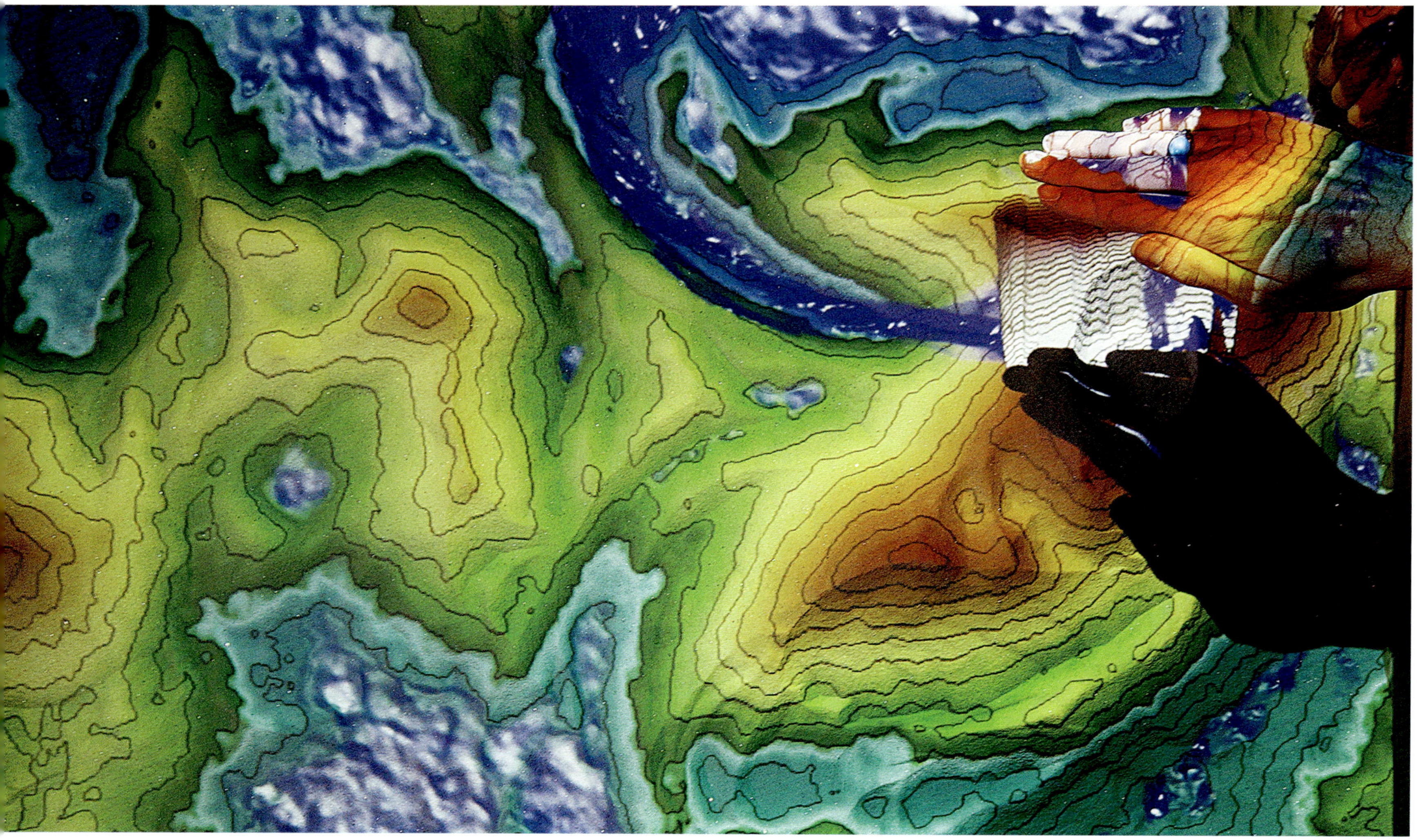

## Water Research

Nebraska sits atop the Ogallala Aquifer, one of the largest freshwater aquifers in the world. In 1887 Nebraska professor of geology Lewis E. Hicks, the first to recognize the importance of Nebraska's groundwater, published "Irrigation in Nebraska" and predicted irrigation would enhance Nebraska agriculture. Today, groundwater and surface irrigation in the state, with over ninety thousand registered, active irrigation wells, supplies water to 8.6 million acres of harvested cropland and pasture. The University is committed to protecting and improving this vital resource through its research initiatives, including the Nebraska Water Center (part of the Robert B. Daugherty Water for Food Global Institute), the High Plains Regional Climate Center, CropWatch, Nebraska Agricultural Water Management Network, and the Center for Advanced Land Management Information Technologies.

Water-related research at the University provides valuable information for policymakers and the public. Projects include groundwater monitoring, watershed planning and management, agricultural irrigation optimization, and stormwater management. The work conducted by UNL faculty, researchers, and students help Nebraska—as well as the nation and the world—meet the challenges of water use now and into the future.

## The E. N. Thompson Forum on World Issues

The E. N. Thompson Forum on World Issues launched in 1988 through funding from the Cooper Foundation; it was originally named the Cooper Foundation–UNL Forum on World Issues. The forum's name was changed in 1990 to honor Cooper Foundation president E. N. "Jack" Thompson, who had conceived of the forum as a way to expose Nebraskans to the people and cultures of other countries and to explore world issues such as poverty, hunger, politics, human rights, religious extremism, terrorism, medical crises, and climate change. Since then, Thompson's visionary series has attracted hundreds of thought-provoking speakers to campus, including Archbishop Desmond Tutu, Mikhail Gorbachev, David Brooks (pictured above), Elie Wiesel, and Maki Mandela. Each year four or five Thompson Forum lectures are held in the Lied Center for Performing Arts (which is now also a presenting partner, along with the Cooper Foundation). A program committee composed of University and community members develop annual themes and choose speakers.

## Nebraska's Midwest Roadside Safety Facility

Drivers around the world can thank the Midwest Roadside Safety Facility, an organization created at UNL in 1990 to study highway safety and design, for making the road a safer place. The facility's leading accomplishment is the SAFER barrier. A breakthrough technology, SAFER (Steel and Foam Energy Reduction barrier) was designed to absorb shock and reduce energy during the impact of a race car. The system is composed of hollow steel tubes attached horizontally via cables to the race track's concrete wall. Sandwiched between the wall and the tubes are layers of a Styrofoam-like material that absorb impact and reduce the chances of driver injury should a race car hit the wall. It also reduces damage to the vehicle, lowering repair costs and getting the car back on the track more quickly. Indianapolis Motor Speedway became the first racetrack to install the technology in 2002, and today all NASCAR and IndyCar tracks use SAFER.

## Cedar Point Biological Station

Nebraska takes advantage of a unique ecological landscape in western Nebraska through Cedar Point Biological Station, a field-based experiential classroom and research area north of Ogallala near Lake McConaughy. Each summer Cedar Point offers courses for undergraduate and graduate students, with housing and dining facilities, a library, classrooms, and research labs on site.

In 1976 the Nature Conservancy purchased 1,280 acres, a tract that is now called Arapaho Prairie, to be managed by Cedar Point expressly for the purpose of conducting research and coursework. Researchers working at Cedar Point have published hundreds of articles, books, theses and dissertations, maps, and presentations about the flora, fauna, and geologic and hydrologic aspects of the region. In 2017 Nebraska alumnus Mark D. Baxa and his wife, Deb, of Charlotte, North Carolina, gave a gift to the NU Foundation to endow scholarships for students wishing to study at Cedar Point and to support construction of a new housing unit there. Baxa studied at Cedar Point during his undergraduate years.

## Drone Research

When it comes to research in the application and use of drones, the sky is literally the limit, and Nebraska researchers are working to develop a multitude of applications for drone use. Journalism professor Matt Waite launched the Drone Journalism Lab, the first of its kind in the nation, in 2011, to explore how journalists can employ drones in their profession. Waite teaches classes and drone "boot camps" on drone operation safety, the legal and ethical issues of drone journalism and the field's best practices, how to coordinate drone operations during a breaking news environment, and how to use drones as part of photographic storytelling.

The Nebraska Intelligent Mobile Unmanned Systems (NIMBUS) Laboratory is leading the country in drone research. Projects include developing drone technology to start, monitor, and collect data on controlled burns and developing software to allow drones to communicate to humans through movement and maintain safe distances from people. Nebraska Extension has produced a number of publications on the uses and aspects of drones in agriculture, and the Daugherty Water for Food Global Institute is using drones to gather data to help farmers make better decisions on when and how to manage complex irrigation systems.

## The Nebraska Lectures

The Nebraska Lectures launched in 2003 under the sponsorship of the Office of Research and Economic Development, the Office of the Chancellor and the Research Council, and the Osher Lifelong Learning Institute. As the chancellor's distinguished lecture series, the Nebraska Lectures are delivered by notable Nebraska faculty from across all disciplines. The series offers a lecture each semester reflecting faculty achievement, research, and creative activity in the arts, the humanities, and the social and physical sciences. Lectures are delivered in an accessible and nontechnical manner to connect the academic community with all Nebraskans. Lecture topics have included the journals of Lewis and Clark, the use of drones in journalism, early childhood education, the HIV/AIDS epidemic, the letters of Willa Cather, and the Dead Sea Scrolls.

## Greenhouse Innovation Center

Nebraska's Greenhouse Innovation Center, which opened in 2015, is working to identify specific traits and characteristics (phenotypes) in plants and then modify or manipulate those traits to induce characteristics, like drought resistance or insect resistance, to improve crop yields. The 45,000-square-foot greenhouse facility is one of just a few in the world with an automated phenotyping system that uses conveyor belts to transport plants to specialized chambers where high-resolution images are captured for research. This enables scientists to closely study plant characteristics and responses to environmental stressors. The phenotyping system significantly advances Nebraska's plant science research and creates private sector collaborations.

Because of the capabilities offered by the center, Nebraska researchers secured a National Science Foundation grant to construct a new instrument to improve the study of plant phenotypes. The multi-wavelength laser imaging and ranging instrument assesses chemical properties and simultaneously measures plant structure in 3-D, providing information about how plant physiology affects function and how function affects plant physiology.

## University of Nebraska State Museum

With towering mammoth skeletons, over one million fossil specimens, and world-class collections, the Nebraska State Museum has inspired thousands of visitors and is a true campus treasure. Founded in 1871, the museum was located in several campus buildings before Morrill Hall was completed in 1927 to house the University's growing paleontological collections.

Researchers at the museum work in the fields of anthropology, botany, entomology, paleontology, parasitology, and zoology. Research initiatives include parasites of mammals, neotropical scarab beetles, and archaeological investigations through the museum's Nebraska Archaeological Survey. The Bessey Herbarium, started in 1874 by Nebraska faculty member Charles Bessey, is part of the museum's Division of Botany. The collection comprises more than 310,000 specimens, including items collected by notable Nebraskans Roscoe Pound, Louise Pound, Willa Cather, and Lawrence Bruner.

Public outreach is a key mission of the museum, and it hosts student fieldtrips, summer camps, and programs like Sunday with a Scientist. The museum also provides social studies and science educational materials. The museum partners with the Nebraska Department of Roads to practice highway salvage paleontology and preserve critical fossil remains from destruction by road construction.

## Holland Computing Center

Nebraska's Holland Computing Center has the fastest computing resources in the state and provides research support for faculty across the University of Nebraska system. Thanks to the Holland Center, Nebraska scientists have roles in two of the world's largest international science projects. Nebraska physicists participated in the initial activities of the Large Hadron Collider project, simulating in miniature the Big Bang that created the universe billions of years ago. As the project moves into its next phases Nebraska scientists are leading efforts to improve the collider so that by 2025 its capacity will be ten times greater, creating significantly more data to detect the rare Higgs boson particle whose existence was first confirmed in 2012. In another project, Holland Center scientists were part of a thousand-member group that first detected gravitational waves that emerged from a collision of black holes 1.3 billion years ago.

## Meat Sciences

Agriculture is Nebraska's No. 1 industry, annually adding more than $25 billion to the state's economy. Nebraska is first in the nation in the export of beef and veal, red meat production, cattle slaughter, and cattle on feed. University of Nebraska research in beef production and products helps drive the entire industry. Faculty engage in improving herd quality through genetics and breeding; feedlot nutrition and grasslands management; herd health and disease management; reduction of livestock impacts on the environment; improved marketing; and beef product development.

Nebraska meat scientists have developed a number of products that increase the value of hogs and cattle by using more parts of the animal. In the 1970s scientist Roger Mandigo developed a process by which less desirable trimmings from meat could be chopped and mixed with salt and water to extract proteins that can bind larger chopped pieces together so they can be shaped into forms. This meat restructuring is the process by which chicken McNuggets and the McRib sandwich were developed by McDonald's. In 2002 scientists from Nebraska and the University of Florida developed several new cuts of meat from beef shoulder, which is a tough and less desirable cut. The most popular new cut is the flat iron steak. The catchy name, combined with the flat iron's tenderness and flavor, made it a huge hit. By 2012 the National Meat Institute said flat iron steaks had brought in around $80 million in sales.

## National Drought Mitigation Center

Drought has been called an insidious natural hazard, as its effects on the environment occur slowly and quietly but with sometimes devastating impact. The National Drought Mitigation Center at Nebraska helps people and institutions across the country plan for and cope with drought, so that drought becomes a matter of risk management rather than crisis management. Established in 1995, the center is part of Nebraska's School of Natural Resources within the Institute of Agriculture and Natural Resources. The center produces the weekly "U.S. Drought Monitor," a valuable tool for policymakers, the agricultural industry, the media, and economists. The publication is a partnership between the center, the U.S. Department of Agriculture, and the National Oceanic and Atmospheric Administration.

The "Drought Impact Reporter," launched in 2005, is the nation's first comprehensive archive of drought impacts, compiling information from media, government agencies, and citizen observers to examine policy responses and track drought's effects on energy use, tourism, agriculture, health, and water supplies. The center conducts extensive education and outreach activities and also publishes guides and plans for agencies, communities, and individuals.

## Parasitology

Nebraska's prominence in the field of parasitology began when Henry Baldwin Ward joined the University's faculty in 1893. The "father of American parasitology," Ward researched parasites of humans and established at Nebraska the first research laboratory to offer graduate study in parasitology. In 1902 Ward was named the first dean of the University of Nebraska College of Medicine, then located in Lincoln. When the college moved to Omaha in 1909, Ward left Nebraska and continued his career at the University of Illinois, where one of his graduate students was Harold W. Manter.

Manter joined the Nebraska faculty in 1927; he was particularly interested in parasites of fish and he traveled widely collecting specimens. Internationally known, Manter described more than three hundred species and sixty-six genera. After his death in 1971, Manter's collection of specimens, literature, and notebooks was donated to the University of Nebraska State Museum, forming the basis of its Division of Parasitology and named the Harold W. Manter Laboratory of Parasitology. The Manter Lab now has more than ninety thousand catalogued records taken from every continent, including ten thousand species of parasites; it is the second-largest collection in the Western Hemisphere. In 2015 the lab received a $500,000 grant from the National Science Foundation to digitize four major collections donated to the lab.

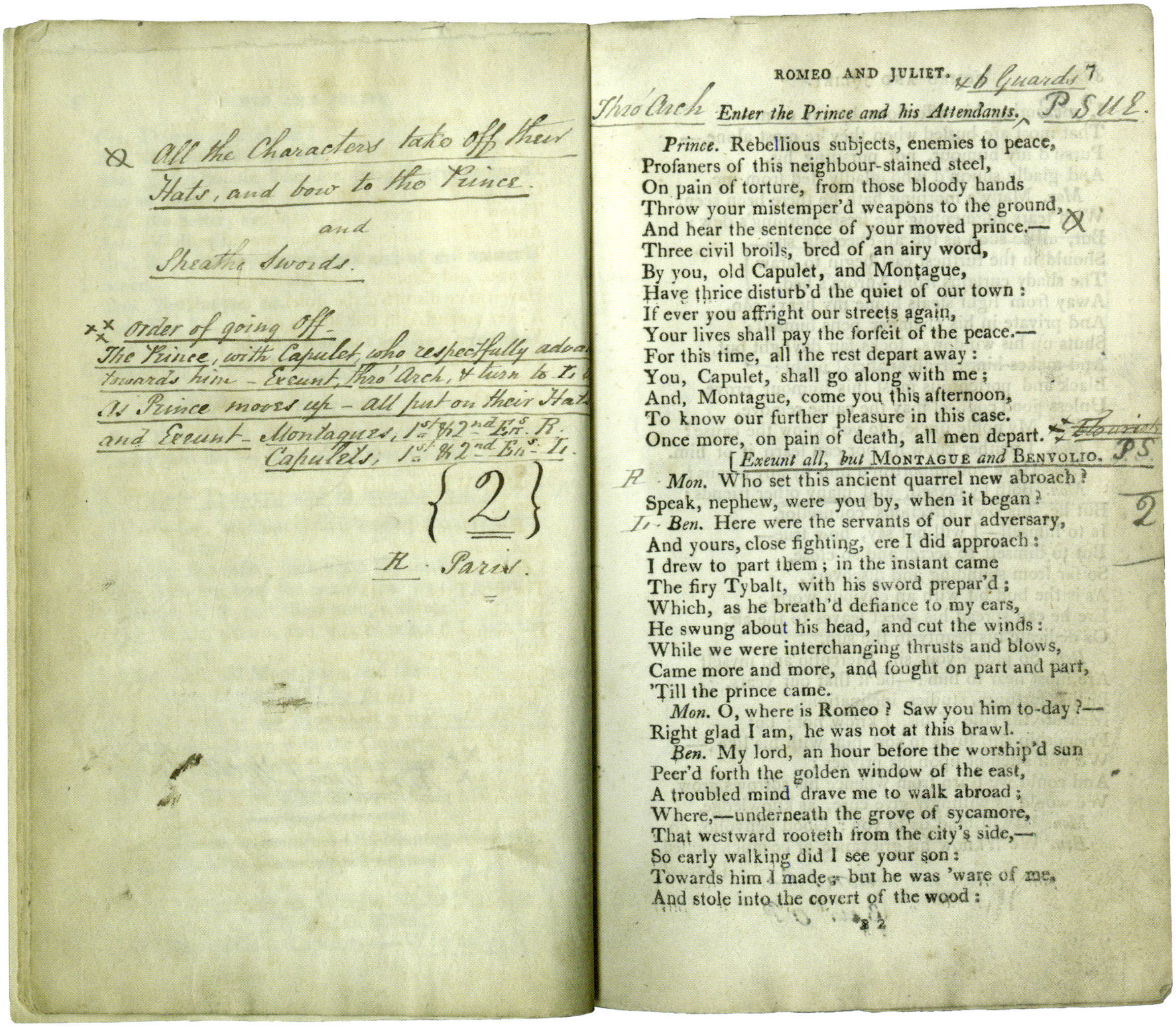

All the Characters take off their Hats, and bow to the Prince.
and
Sheathe Swords.

Order of going Off.
The Prince, with Capulet, who respectfully advances towards him – Exeunt, Thro' Arch, & turn to the
As Prince moves up – all put on their Hats and Exeunt – Montagues, 1st & 2nd En. R.
Capulets, 1st & 2nd En. L.

{2}

R. Paris.

ROMEO AND JULIET.

Thro' Arch Enter the Prince and his Attendants. & 6 Guards P.S. U.E.

*Prince.* Rebellious subjects, enemies to peace,
Profaners of this neighbour-stained steel,
On pain of torture, from those bloody hands
Throw your mistemper'd weapons to the ground,
And hear the sentence of your moved prince.—
Three civil broils, bred of an airy word,
By you, old Capulet, and Montague,
Have thrice disturb'd the quiet of our town:
If ever you affright our streets again,
Your lives shall pay the forfeit of the peace.—
For this time, all the rest depart away:
You, Capulet, shall go along with me;
And, Montague, come you this afternoon,
To know our further pleasure in this case.
Once more, on pain of death, all men depart.
[*Exeunt all, but* MONTAGUE *and* BENVOLIO. P.S.
*Mon.* Who set this ancient quarrel new abroach?
Speak, nephew, were you by, when it began?
*Ben.* Here were the servants of our adversary,
And yours, close fighting, ere I did approach:
I drew to part them; in the instant came
The firy Tybalt, with his sword prepar'd;
Which, as he breath'd defiance to my ears,
He swung about his head, and cut the winds:
While we were interchanging thrusts and blows,
Came more and more, and fought on part and part,
'Till the prince came.
*Mon.* O, where is Romeo? Saw you him to-day?—
Right glad I am, he was not at this brawl.
*Ben.* My lord, an hour before the worship'd sun
Peer'd forth the golden window of the east,
A troubled mind drave me to walk abroad;
Where,—underneath the grove of sycamore,
That westward rooteth from the city's side,—
So early walking did I see your son:
Towards him I made; but he was 'ware of me,
And stole into the covert of the wood:

## Shakespeare Collection

Among the many objects, documents, and collections held by the Archives & Special Collections of the UNL Libraries is a group of materials related to Shakespeare and his works. The premiere volume in the collection is the Shakespeare First Folio, which was published in 1623 as the first collected edition of his plays. There are only about 230 known copies of the First Folio, which contains thirty-six of Shakespeare's plays, including some that were never published before publication of the folio, including "Macbeth" and "Julius Caesar." Other works in the Shakespeare collection include copies of the 1674 version of "Macbeth," a circa-1686 edition of "Julius Caesar," and a 1703 "Hamlet."

The Shakespeare First Folio was donated to University Libraries in 1991 as its two millionth volume, by Sidney Johnsen Wayland. In 1971 Wayland's late father, Johnny Johnsen, the founder of Nebraska Book Company, donated the libraries' one-millionth volume, a 1542 copy of *The Works of Geoffrey Chaucer.* A first edition copy of Walt Whitman's "Leaves of Grass," published in 1855, is the libraries' three-millionth volume.

## Polar Sciences/ANDRILL

Clues about climate change can be discerned from studying past climate extremes, and a valuable source of historical climate information can be found in ice core samples. Nebraska scientists have been working in the field of polar ice research since the 1950s, and current research continues under ANDRILL. Short for Antarctic Geological Drilling, ANDRILL is a multinational collaboration of more than two hundred researchers from eight countries who drill and recover ice cores whose layers hold evidence of millions of years of earth history. Nebraska geoscientists have successfully extracted and examined a 3,375-foot-long sample of rock from beneath Antarctica's McMurdo Sound, giving researchers access to sediment deposited between twenty million and fourteen million years ago. By analyzing the sediments, scientists can reconstruct shifts in water temperatures, ice coverage, and sea levels throughout that period.

## Center for Great Plains Studies

Established in 1976, the Center for Great Plains Studies fosters the study and appreciation of the people, cultures, and environment of the North American Great Plains. The only academic center devoted to the study of this region, the center operates the Plains Humanities Alliance, offers graduate and undergraduate programs of study, publishes the journals *Great Plains Quarterly* and *Great Plains Research*, and sponsors public lectures and interdisciplinary symposia. Current focus areas of scholars and fellows affiliated with the center are ecotourism, the history of homesteading, and Native American history and culture. Among the center's most iconic projects was the publication of the *Complete Journals of Lewis and Clark*, a thirteen-volume annotated edition of the explorers' journals, edited by Gary Moulton and published by the University of Nebraska Press from 1983 to 2001.

The center is also home to the Great Plains Art Museum, which opened in 1981. The foundation of the museum is the Christlieb Collection of western art, an important collection of sculpture, works on paper, drawings, photographs, paintings, and other works donated by John and Elizabeth Christlieb.

## Buffett Early Childhood Institute

Created in 2011 with a gift from Omaha philanthropist Susie Buffett, the Buffett Early Childhood Institute draws on research and expertise from the four University of Nebraska campuses. The institute works to transform the care and education of at-risk children from birth to age eight and to assist their families. The institute's vision is to make Nebraska the best place in the nation to be a baby. Decades of research have shown that the experiences of the early years have a major impact on children's success in school and life. Among the institute's goals are to increase opportunities for young children to learn and eliminate income-based and race-based achievement gaps by the end of third grade.

# No Place Like Nebraska

## CAMPUS BUILDINGS AND LANDMARKS

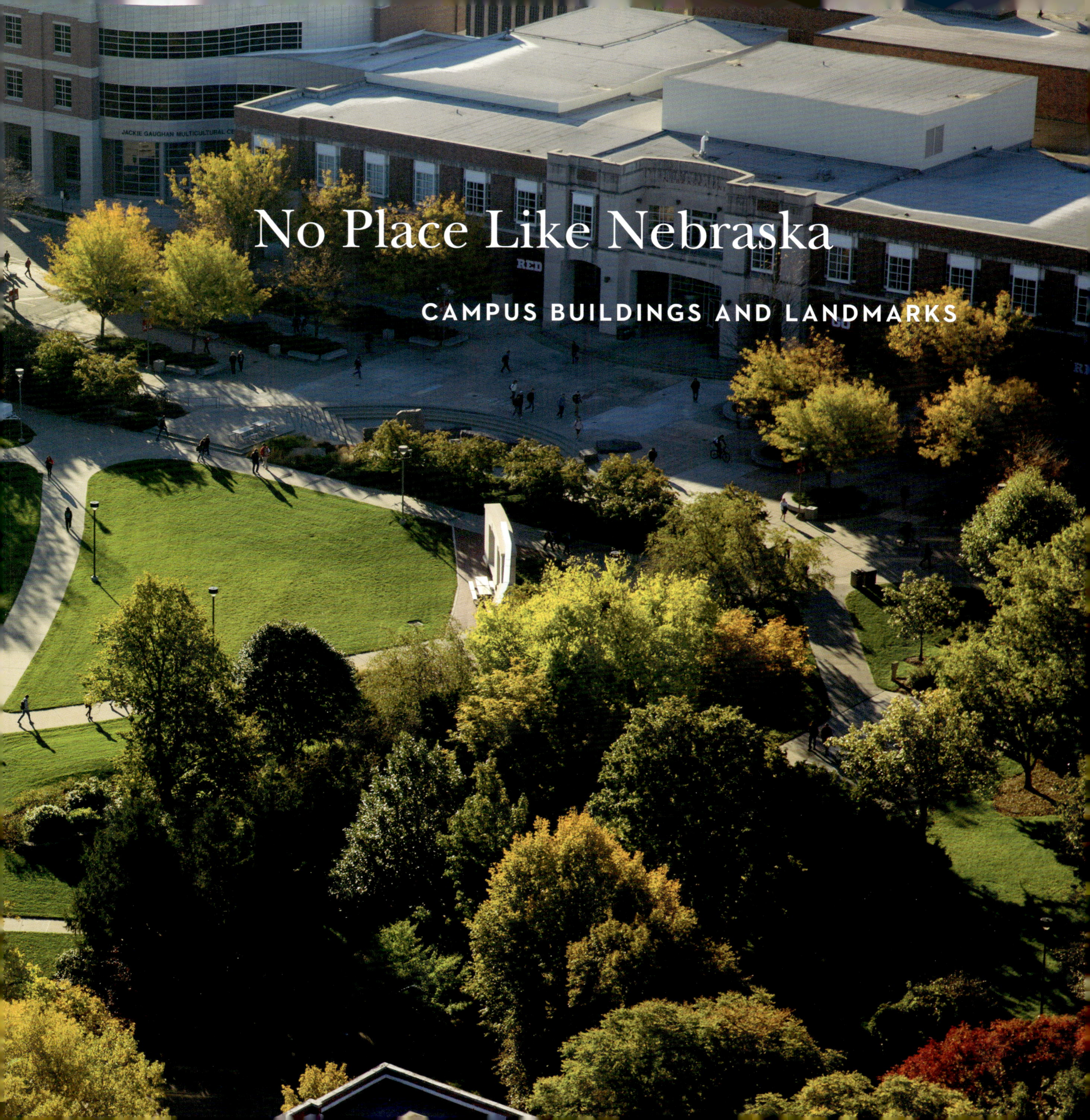

Every Husker has memories of campus: eating ice cream at the Dairy Store, studying at Love or Thompson library, trying to find all the letters of the alphabet in the "Old Glory" sculpture, hearing the bell tower between classes, spending time with friends in dorm rooms or one of the student unions, long days in classrooms and laboratories. Buildings and structures help tell the University's story.

The University of Nebraska's architectural styles and location choices reflect changing eras and academic priorities. Buildings have been constructed during times of plenty and in response to enrollment growth—like the flurry of building after World War II when enrollment doubled, or again in the 1960s and 1970s in the form of student housing, and another student housing boom after 2001. Buildings have been erected to house new or expanding academic and research needs and they have been purposely built for natural history and art museums, music halls, theaters, or to accommodate Nebraska's athletic teams.

Many buildings carry the names of donors who made construction possible or whose contributions deserve recognition. These include Othmer Hall (named for Donald F. Othmer, a 1924 graduate of UNL and a noted chemical engineer and professor; funding for the engineering building came from the estate of his widow, Mildred Topp Othmer, a 1928 UNL graduate), the Van Brunt Visitors Center (named after Winslow and Irene Van Brunt, 1924 graduates of UNL and both active members of the Nebraska Alumni Association during their lives), and the Adele Hall Learning Commons (named in honor of 1953 alumna, Lincoln native, and lifelong Husker Adele Coryell Hall).

Other buildings are named for faculty or administrators whose work has had a significant influence on the university: Kiesselbach Crops Research Laboratory (named in honor of Theodore Kiesselbach, a Nebraska alumnus and Agronomy Department faculty member who was world renowned for his research in corn), Ferguson Hall (named for Olin J. Ferguson, a native Nebraskan and 1903 alumnus who worked at General Electric

before returning to Nebraska in 1912 to serve as chair of the Electrical Engineering Department and later as dean of the College of Engineering), and Robert E. Knoll Residential Center (honoring Knoll, who served as a faculty member in the Department of English for forty years and authored *Prairie University: A History of the University of Nebraska*).

While buildings are important landmarks, the people who use those buildings and the buildings' purposes define the spaces. As campus needs have changed, buildings have been adapted or razed and new buildings have been constructed. As the University moves into Nebraska Innovation Campus with an eye toward meeting future research challenges, the University's footprint enlarges. The three campuses of UNL will continue to transform, change, and grow, all the while remaining the home of the Huskers and reminding us that there is no place like Nebraska.

CONNECT
THE MILL

## University Hall

The University campus's first building was University Hall, situated on a small hill north of downtown Lincoln. Four stories tall and designed in a Franco Italianate style, the building was more impressive than the city's new state capitol building and it stood out in the small prairie town of only 2,500 people. University Hall included a chapel; twenty recitation rooms; rooms for various literary societies, music, and painting; a room for housing geological, botanical, and biological specimens; a laboratory; an armory; a ladies' reception room; and a printing office. Three workers died during the building's construction, and the use of low-quality materials caused many structural failures during University Hall's lifespan. The building was renovated numerous times and finally demolished in 1948. Its original bell lives on in the garden of the Wick Alumni Center.

## East Campus Mall

Campus maps from as early as 1911 show that buildings on East Campus were situated along a mall, although early building locations may have predated the formal mall plan. Buildings such as the 1899 Experiment Station (now Ag Communications) and Agriculture Hall were sited along platted roadways, with sidewalks and greenspaces. In 1909 W. H. Dunman was hired as the Farm Campus gardener; he eventually contributed to City Campus landscaping. An Englishman, Dunman had worked at Sandringham, the Norfolk estate of the Prince of Wales, later King Edward VII. Dunman's knowledge of English border gardens is evident. Old photographs reveal the use of cannas and herbaceous perennials. Dunman also won awards for developing iris and other plants. Other buildings (Plant Industry, now Entomology Hall, and the original Home Economics Building) were added; Agricultural Engineering (now Chase Hall) anchored the mall's north end.

## Agricultural Communications

Agricultural Communications, the oldest building on East Campus, was built in 1899 as the Agriculture Experiment Station. Originally the building's first floor housed experiment station offices, with upper levels used for classrooms and laboratories. Other units included the Department of Agricultural Chemistry, a soil laboratory, an entomology laboratory, and horticultural workrooms and greenhouses. The station's library, which had been entrusted to the care of the University librarian, was housed in the building. The building was once connected to a greenhouse that extended south. Renovated in 1959, Agricultural Communications is the only remaining nineteenth-century building on East Campus.

## Howard L. Hawks Hall

Howard L. Hawks Hall, at 240,000 square feet, is the largest academic building project in recent campus history. Named in honor of an Omaha businessman, philanthropist, and current Regent, Hawks Hall is the home of the College of Business. The college relocated into the $84 million building in fall 2017. Hawks Hall features experiential learning spaces and high-tech classrooms, with eight cluster classrooms and eight case-style classrooms to foster positive group dynamics so students can seamlessly transition between lecture-style presentations and small group projects. The 1,700-square-foot College of Business Husker Shop is a partnership with Nebraska Athletics and merchandiser Fanatics, where students manage a Husker fan shop within the academic space. The state-of-the-art Trading Room, a simulated stock trading area, provides a real-time environment for students to experience what it is like to work in finance.

## Sheldon Museum of Art

The elegant travertine and glass Sheldon Museum of Art was designed by architect Philip Johnson with a contemporary, sleek design and was funded by gifts from Frances Sheldon and her brother, A. Bromley Sheldon. Prior to the Sheldon's opening in 1963, the University's art museum was housed in Morrill Hall, the University's natural history museum. Construction began in 1961, and Italian stone artisans traveled to Lincoln to supervise the placement of the museum's travertine marble, which had been cut and numbered in Italy. The museum's interior centers around

a windowed great hall, which spans the building's width east to west and allows visitors to see through the space. A dramatic bridge and double staircase dominate the great hall, linking the upper galleries. The building is listed on the National Register of Historic Places and is among the University's most prominent and well-known landmark structures.

The museum houses the collections of both the Sheldon Art Association, founded in 1888, and the University of Nebraska. Together the collections comprise more than 12,500 works in diverse media, and the Sheldon is considered to be among the finest university art museums in the country. The museum's comprehensive collection of American art includes prominent holdings of nineteenth-century landscape and still life, American impressionism, early modernism, geometric abstraction, abstract expressionism, pop, minimalism, and contemporary art. Artists include Edward Hopper, Georgia O'Keeffe, Andy Warhol, Mark Rothko, and Aaron Douglas.

More than thirty of Sheldon's monumental sculptures are exhibited throughout the University's City and East Campuses, including works by Jun Kaneko, Claes Oldenburg, and Richard Serra. The Sheldon hosts programs for students from elementary school to college and sponsors traveling exhibits throughout the state. The museum has always been, and remains, free and open to the public, thanks to support from the Sheldon Art Association, the museum's donors, and the University.

## Architecture Hall

Nebraska's iconic Architecture Hall was added to the National Register of Historic Places in 1975. The sole remaining nineteenth-century building on City Campus, Architecture Hall links the University's early years with the contemporary institution. Construction on Architecture Hall began in 1892, but an economic recession delayed its completion and the building stood empty, roofed but with no door, until the Nebraska Legislature reconvened in 1895 and appropriated the final construction funds. The building housed the University library (until Love Library opened in 1945) along with an art gallery, classrooms, and space for the Nebraska State Historical Society. The building was constructed with more care than earlier campus buildings, having a slate roof, clerestory windows, and steel beams and girders for fire resistance. Though Architecture Hall was extensively renovated from 1985 to 1987, with a multistory glass "link" connecting it to the former Law College to the west, its exterior has remained essentially unchanged.

## Lied Center for Performing Arts

The Lied Center is a space where students and community members engage with world leaders, a setting where new artistic works are created and developed, a place where Nebraskans can relate to and learn from the greatest artistic minds of our time, and a place where thousands have experienced the arts for the very first time. The Lied Center was funded in the early 1980s by a $10 million matching grant from the Lied Foundation Trust, to honor 1927 University graduate Ernst F. Lied's parents, Ernst M. and Ida K. Lied. The Lied Foundation also funded the Lied Commons addition in 2012. Durward "Woody" Varner, former NU president and Lied Foundation CEO, spearheaded the efforts to create this performing arts center to serve not only the University and Lincoln, but the entire state.

As construction of the Lied Center neared completion, Nebraska native, University graduate, and late-night television legend Johnny Carson funded a secondary black box performance space for smaller-scale community and

experimental productions—The Johnny Carson Theater. Completed in 1989, the Lied Center is a state-of-the-art performing arts venue designed to attract, entertain, and inspire a statewide audience. Established as "Nebraska's Home for the Arts," the Lied Center is recognized as one of the top one hundred performing arts centers in the world. Artists at the Lied have ranged from Yo-Yo Ma and Itzhak Perlman to Wynton Marsalis, the American Ballet Theatre, and the St. Louis Symphony Orchestra.

## Don L. Love Memorial Library and Adele Coryell Hall Learning Commons

Ground was broken for a new university library in spring 1941 after the original library (housed in what is now known as Architecture Hall) outgrew its space. A gift from the estate of Lincoln businessman and mayor Don L. Love assured the building's construction. In 1943, before the library was opened to students, the U.S. Army took possession of the building—mostly a roofed shell with heat and water—for use as a barracks. Love opened as a library in fall 1945 and was the largest building on campus. It was designed to house eight hundred thousand volumes, had six large reading rooms with seating for nearly 1,000 people, and featured more than fifty study rooms for faculty and graduate students. A large auditorium seated 360 and a student lounge for socializing was incorporated into the original plan. Love's distinctive cupola has become a campus icon.

In 1972 an addition was constructed on the north side of the building, altering the distinctive entry area and disrupting the quadrangle. Pedestrians' east-west campus route was preserved as Love North was connected to Love South by an enclosed second floor "link." In 2016 Love North was renovated into the Adele Hall Learning Commons, a $10 million, 30,000-square-foot space designed to promote scholarship and collaboration. The Learning Commons

includes a café/coffee shop, eighteen study rooms, numerous seating areas, a testing center, staffed help stations, and a video-creation studio. The project was made possible through nearly $7 million in private gifts. A leadership gift was made by the family of Donald J. Hall, chairman of Hallmark Cards Inc. of Kansas City, in memory of the late Adele Coryell Hall, a Lincoln native and 1953 graduate. Other donors included alumni Kit and Dick Schmoker of Edina, Minnesota; Tom and Candy Henning of Lincoln; and Barbara Arnold MD of Sacramento, California.

## Agriculture Hall

Agriculture Hall is the administrative home to the Institute of Agriculture and Natural Resources and anchors the southwest corner of the East Campus Mall. Construction of Agriculture Hall began in 1904 and the building was dedicated in 1906. Planned as a classroom building, Ag Hall also housed the library materials formerly housed in the Agriculture Experiment Station building. Library materials remained in Agriculture Hall until the construction of C. Y. Thompson Library. The building was designed by Ferdinand Fiske, an important early Lincoln architect. Fiske also designed the Women's Building, later called Home Economics, north of Ag Hall. That building was demolished in the 1960s.

## Mary Riepma Ross Media Arts Center

The Mary Riepma Ross Media Arts Center is a thriving theater celebrating film as an art form. The Ross theater screens diverse films, including innovative and experimental American and foreign films, classic films, and documentaries. Part of the Van Brunt Visitors Center, the Ross opened in its current form in 2003. Its roots, however, stretch back nearly fifty years to the original Sheldon Film Theater, founded by Norman Geske, the inaugural director of the Sheldon Memorial Art Gallery (now Sheldon Museum of Art.) Geske, who died in 2014, considered film the defining art medium of the twentieth century, and he included an auditorium and film program in the Sheldon's original development plan. In 1990 Nebraska graduate Mary Riepma Ross pledged a $3.5 million estate gift toward the construction of a theater facility separate and distinct from the Sheldon, and the Mary Riepma Ross Film Theater was born.

The Ross is home to the Johnny Carson School of Theatre and Film's film and new media production emphasis, which prepares students for careers in the film and television industry, and has an archival quality film/video storage facility that houses some two thousand titles including the UNL Film Studies collection. Ross left an additional $7.7 million to the University of Nebraska Foundation to endow the Ross Media Arts Center after her death in 2013 at age 102, ensuring that the Ross will continue to be a vibrant part of the Lincoln and state arts scene.

## Dairy Store

Dishing up tens of thousands of scoops of ice cream every year, the Dairy Store is a campus landmark. The Dairy Store opened in the Dairy Industry building in 1917 under the name Varsity Dairy; it provided dairy products for residence halls and offered all-you-can-drink milk for a nickel to anyone who came with his or her own cup. Dairy Industry was renamed H. C. Filley Hall in 1972 to honor a longtime faculty member in agricultural economics. The Dairy Store and the dairy plant provide an important learning opportunity for Nebraska's food science students to conduct research, develop products, and prepare for future careers in the food industry.

## Maxwell Arboretum

Maxwell Arboretum, located on East Campus, is a signature garden for the University and a premier site of the Nebraska Statewide Arboretum. The twelve-acre arboretum exhibits both native and exotic species, herbaceous perennial gardens, and woody plants. Special collections include hostas, irises, oaks, lilacs, rhododendrons, and a prairie that showcases native grasses. The regents approved the proposed Maxwell Arboretum in 1967 after a student suggested the area be set aside from development or destruction and be named after Earl G. Maxwell.

A native of Indiana, Maxwell (1884–1966) earned a master's degree from the University of Nebraska in 1915. He taught at the university from 1915 to 1917 and then became the first extension agent for Douglas County, a position he held for twelve years. From 1934 to his retirement in 1952 Maxwell served as the state extension forester, overseeing programs through which more than twenty million trees were distributed and planted throughout Nebraska. Maxwell was intensely interested in finding trees and shrubs that could thrive in Nebraska's varied and sometimes harsh climate, and the University continues to add new species to the Maxwell Arboretum

## International Quilt Study Center & Museum

Established in 1997, the International Quilt Study Center & Museum houses the largest public collection of quilts in the world. The original collection was owned by and donated to Nebraska by Ardis and Robert James, whose collection comprised more than one thousand quilts. The center originally was housed in a climate-controlled space in the Home Economics building on East Campus, with quilts exhibited at various galleries across campus or loaned to museums elsewhere. A gift from the James family and private fundraising, including donations from more than 130 quilt guilds and quilt organizations in four countries, enabled construction of the 37,000-square foot Quilt Museum, which opened in 2008. The collection comprises more than six thousand quilts, representing fifty countries and over four hundred years of history. The International Quilt Study Center & Museum is on the leading edge of quilt studies, and the Department of Textiles, Merchandising, and Fashion Design offers a master's degree with an emphasis in quilt studies, the only such program in the world.

Jeff Davis & Daughter
Master I Am Free

## Morrill Hall

Unlike many Morrill Halls found on land grant campuses across the country, Nebraska's is named not for U.S. legislator and namesake of the Morrill Act, Justin Morrill, but for Charles Morrill, a regent, friend of the University, and benefactor. Charles Morrill underwrote many of the archaeological digs that were led by museum director Erwin H. Barbour and undertaken in western Nebraska beginning in 1892. Also known as Elephant Hall, Morrill Hall opened in 1927 and today houses the University of Nebraska State Museum and its collection of more than one million specimens. Elephant Hall was developed as the museum's grand exhibit space to showcase fossil remains of prehistoric mammals, including the world's largest wooly mammoth skeleton on exhibit. The building has undergone numerous renovations, including one of its fourth floor into new exhibit space called Cherish Nebraska. The new space celebrates the state's natural heritage, which has been shaped over the millennia by geological and human forces. Other features of Morrill Hall include Mueller Planetarium and permanent exhibits that showcase Nebraska's Native and indigenous people and the extensive collections of Nebraska's paleontology.

## Ashfall Fossil Beds State Historical Park

Nebraska paleontologist Mike Voorhies made the discovery of a lifetime in 1971 when he spotted the fossil skull of an ancient baby rhinoceros poking from the wall of a ravine near Royal in northeast Nebraska. The intact skull led Voorhies to the eventual discovery of hundreds of fossil remains at the site. The animals near Royal died about twelve million years ago with the eruption of a volcano hundreds of miles west, sending a one-to-two-foot deep blanket of ash across a large area. The animals survived the ashfall, but inhalation of ash damaged their lungs and they died at this ancient waterhole. The ash covered their bodies and preserved the remains. Approximately twenty mammal species, including rhinos, camels, and three-toed horses, plus birds and turtles are represented among the hundreds of skeletons.

In 1991 Ashfall Fossil Beds State Historical Park opened, a joint project of the University of Nebraska State Museum and the Nebraska Game and Parks Commission. Open to the public during the summer, this 360-acre National Natural Landmark includes a visitors' center and two large covered barns where visitors can see the skeletons in situ and watch scientists at work. Many of the park's amenities were built thanks to the generous donation of the Theodore F. and Claire M. Hubbard Family Foundation of Omaha, whose gifts paid for construction of the Hubbard Rhino Barn, artwork, and other facilities. Voorhies and others from the University of Nebraska State Museum continue to excavate the site. Dozens of students from across the nation and around the world research Ashfall's geology and paleontology, and many University of Nebraska students have gained practical field research experience as paleontological interns at the site.

B5
Troy
B4
Amanda

## Nebraska Unions

The Nebraska Unions are hubs of activity for students and student-led organizations, and the City Campus Nebraska Union is truly a student-driven building. Student president and later editor of the *Daily Nebraskan* Jack Fischer spearheaded efforts to lobby and secure Public Works Administration funds to use in constructing a building for student social use. The Public Works Administration provided 45 percent of the funding for the new building; the remainder was paid for with a $3-a-semester student fee. The union was an elegant addition to a campus still recovering from the Great Depression when it opened in 1938. Aside from Memorial Stadium, few campus buildings have undergone more renovation or expansion. Major additions were built in 1959, 1969, and 1999, each time moving the building farther north and enlarging its footprint.

EBRASKA UNION

The south facade on R Street, however, has remained unchanged. The Broyhill Fountain, constructed in 1969 as a memorial to a student killed in a car accident, was relocated and redesigned as part of the 1999 addition, becoming the focal point of the North Union Plaza.

The Nebraska East Union opened January 17, 1977. The diamond-shaped building was the culmination of decades of student petitions to create union facilities on East Campus. When a temporary union opened in the East Campus Student Activities Building in 1947, the grand opening included a performance by a student magician, Johnny Carson. The East Union building includes a ballroom, a cafeteria, a bowling alley, a bookstore, and meeting rooms and office spaces; a major renovation is underway.

The Home of
NEBRASKA BOWLING
12 TIME
NATIONAL CHAMPIONS
1990 1999 2013
1991 2001 2015
1995 2004
1996 2005
1997 2009

## Loeffel Meats Laboratory

Loeffel Meats Laboratory carries the name of a faculty member hired in 1919 on the promise that a modern meat research laboratory would be built. The building was erected, but not until 1954. William Loeffel worked in the new building until his retirement in 1959 and the building was renamed in his honor in 1967. The building contained a slaughter floor, butchering equipment, a smokehouse, labs, and classrooms and was considered one of the best meat labs in the country when it opened. In 1968 Nebraska opened Marvel Baker Hall for the Animal Sciences Department. In 1988 a new Animal Sciences building was constructed, connecting Baker and Loeffel Halls. At the Meats Laboratory students in the Animal Science Department now process beef, pork, turkey, and lamb that is available for sale to the public.

## Mueller Tower

The chimes of Mueller Tower are a daily part of City Campus life. Dedicated during homecoming festivities in 1949, Mueller Tower was the gift of Ralph Mueller (1877–1966), an 1898 graduate. Mueller also received an honorary degree from Nebraska in 1943. Mueller was a successful manufacturer of materials used in electronics, and when approached about making a donation to the University, he donated $90,000 toward a bell tower. (Mueller also donated funds to build the Mueller Planetarium in Morrill Hall and to restore the "old Iron Gates," which are part of the Columns east of Memorial Stadium.) Eighty-four feet tall, the tower was designed by architecture student George Kuska and features a modern, art deco look with stylized ears of corn around the top, rather than Mueller's desired design of a building in the shape of an ear of corn. Today the tower contains an electronic broadcast system that can be controlled remotely and has a repertoire of about 750 songs.

## Prem S. Paul Research Center at Whittier School

After Lincoln Public Schools closed Whittier Junior High, the nation's first junior high school, the University of Nebraska Foundation purchased the building in 1983. In 2007 the Board of Regents approved a $24 million project to renovate the building into space for use by interdisciplinary research programs and the University's child care center. The restoration was done with an eye toward preserving and restoring the building's magnificent architecture, including grand staircases, terra cotta exteriors, and marble flooring. Large windows that open into courtyards provide natural daylight; geothermal energy provides heating and cooling.

The building houses several major University research programs including the Center for Children, Youth, Families, and Schools; the Nebraska Center for Energy Sciences; the Nebraska Transportation Center; the Midwest Roadside Safety Facility; the Social and Behavioral Sciences Research Consortium; and the Computational Science Initiative. In fall 2016 the building was renamed to honor the late Prem S. Paul, who served as vice chancellor for research and economic development from 2001 until his death in 2016. During Paul's tenure, Nebraska's research funding grew to an all-time high of $146.9 million. Paul was a strong advocate for interdisciplinary research and led the establishment of centers that merged disciplines, including the Nebraska Center for Energy Sciences Research, the Center for Brain, Biology and Behavior, the Carson Center for Emerging Media Arts, the Ken Morrison Life Sciences Research Center, the Extreme Light Laboratory, and the Central Plains Research Data Center.

## Temple Building

Few buildings have elicited as much controversy as Temple, mostly due to the source of its funding. In the early 1900s Chancellor Benjamin Andrews secured $66,666.66 from John D. Rockefeller Jr., a personal friend, to help finance a much-needed student activities building. In populist Nebraska, though, Rockefeller money was anathema, especially to William Jennings Bryan, who orated against the plan. Nevertheless, Andrews successfully raised the necessary matching funds. He had already personally purchased and donated land for the building, which was across the street from the original campus—the first time the University crept past its original boundaries. Construction was completed by 1908, and today Temple houses University Theatre.

## Lester F. Larsen Tractor Test and Power Museum

When tractors and mechanized agriculture equipment began to be widely used in the early 1900s, farmers needed a way to ensure the equipment delivered what manufacturers promised. The Nebraska Legislature enacted a law that required all tractors sold in Nebraska to be certified by the University, and the Tractor Test Laboratory was opened in 1919 to achieve that goal. Over the years thousands of tractors have been tested in the lab and on the adjacent test track. In 1980 the lab building was designated a historic site by the American Society of Agricultural Engineers. Tractor Test director Lester Larsen, who retired in 1975 after thirty-nine years of service, had collected about forty vintage tractors. Larsen's collection was moved into the original Tractor Lab, and the University of Nebraska State Museum agreed to incorporate the tractor museum as an adjunct facility. In 1998 the museum was formally dedicated. A historic building constructed by Behlen Manufacturing Company of Columbus, Nebraska, that had survived a nuclear test explosion in New Mexico, became a site for tractor restorations. Among the most significant restorations undertaken by the student-run Tractor Restoration Club include a 1945 Allis Chalmers Model C, used to clear land on the last homestead claim in the United States that was filed in 1974 in Alaska. The tractor is now part of a museum exhibit at Homestead National Monument near Beatrice.

## Brace Laboratory of Physics

Brace Laboratory opened in 1906 and was named for a rising faculty star, DeWitt Bristol Brace, the chairman of the Physics Department, who died just months before the building was completed. In 1965 Behlen Laboratory was appended to Brace Laboratory's west side, and Brace and Behlen were extensively renovated in 2014 and 2016, respectively. The renovation of Brace Hall, which in 2015 won an award from the Preservation Association of Lincoln, converted the building into an innovative teaching facility. It now houses four life sciences laboratories and support space; a 186-seat auditorium; four classrooms; the Technology Transforming Teaching (T3) classroom; and space that will allow Information Technology Services employees to provide classroom and learning support.

Behlen's renovation transformed it into a flexible and modern research facility with six dedicated lab spaces, conference rooms, and support areas. Alongside ongoing exploration in Nebraska's Extreme Light Laboratory—which is located in Behlen's basement and sub-basement—the new design allows for research projects that demand higher levels of security, such as those funded by the U.S. Department of Defense.

## The Columns and Athletics Hall of Fame

Originally part of Omaha's Burlington Depot, the Columns were relocated to Lincoln and placed between Memorial Stadium and the Coliseum in 1930. The Old Iron Gates were part of the fence that encircled the original campus from 1892 to 1922. Although the fence was removed and later sold to Wyuka Cemetery in Lincoln, the gates stood for several more years until they, too, were removed. Students asked for their return, and in 1942 they were erected north of the new Nebraska Union, only to be removed again in 1947. The Nebraska Alumni Association began another effort to restore the gates to campus, and a donation by alumnus Ralph Mueller underwrote the restoration and placement of the gates near the Columns in 1955.

Alumna Adelloyd Whiting Williams's comments now grace a plaque honoring the gates: "These gates are the last link between the old and new University. May they serve as a memorial to the past and a gateway to the future." In 2015, following extensive expansion of the east facade of Memorial Stadium, the Nebraska Athletics Department created the Nebraska Athletics Hall of Fame plaza and located it on a renovated walkway stretching from the Columns to the Coliseum. The inaugural hall of fame class, announced in 2015, included twenty-two distinguished student-athletes, one from each sport in which Nebraska fields a team. A new Huskers hall of fame class is selected annually. The 2018 class included coaches for the first time by inducting Bob Devaney and Tom Osborne.

## C. Y. Thompson Library

The Agricultural Library was originally housed in Agriculture Hall, but the library space became so overtaxed that materials were stored in the basement, the attic, and even in Love Library. C. Y. Thompson Library was approved in 1961 and local architecture firm Clark and Enersen designed the library as a modern interpretation of a classic Greek temple with piers and glass. Dedicated in 1966, the library is named for Charles Yoder Thompson, a prominent agricultural leader and four-term president of the University Board of Regents. C. Y. Thompson is scheduled for major renovation that will reflect contemporary student and faculty needs for digitally accessed information, individual and collaborative study and meeting spaces, and multidiscipline book collections. While digital access will be emphasized, a "power library" of about sixty thousand volumes will remain in the building.

## Trailside Museum of Natural History

The Trailside Museum, housed in the original army theater building at Nebraska's Fort Robinson State Park near Harrison, opened on July 3, 1961, as a branch museum of the University of Nebraska State Museum. The museum is located in the fossil-rich Pine Ridge region and contains exhibits of local prehistoric finds collected by the University since 1891. The museum's most renowned exhibit is the fossil remains of two mammoths that died with their tusks locked in combat. The dueling mammoths died ten thousand years ago north of present-day Crawford and were discovered in 1962.

## Hardin Hall

The Nebraska Center for Continuing Education opened in 1961 as a facility for the University to host conferences, institutes, workshops, and seminars for all Nebraskans. The center included a 98-room hotel, a six-hundred-seat auditorium, numerous classrooms in the adjacent youth facility, an eight-hundred-seat banquet hall, and a restaurant and cafeteria. While the center was initially popular and well-used, the hotel and food service operations were spotty and eventually began to lose money. In 2003 the center was completely gutted and repurposed into office, research, and classroom space for the School of Natural Resources, then rededicated in 2006. In 1961 the regents had proposed naming the building in honor of former Nebraska chancellor Clifford Hardin, due to his efforts to build the center. He deferred the honor, but thirty-three years later, in 1994, it was belatedly bestowed. Hardin was Nebraska's youngest chancellor when he was installed in 1954; he served until 1969 when he joined the Nixon administration to serve as U.S. Secretary of Agriculture until 1971. Hardin died in 2010 at the age of ninety-four.

## Esther L. Kauffman Academic Residential Center

When the Esther S. Kauffman Academic Residential Center opened in 2001, it was the first new student housing project at Nebraska in more than twenty years. Located in the heart of City Campus, the Kauffman Center was financed through a gift from Carole and Ed McVaney in honor of Carole's mother, Esther Kauffman. The Kauffman Center's living quarters include housing for all undergraduate students in the Jeffrey S. Raikes School of Computer Science and Management, as well as apartments for visiting faculty and guest lecturers. The building is designed to enhance the team approach to problem solving by encouraging interaction and collaboration among the school's students, faculty, and industry leaders. The center features the latest technology-equipped classrooms, meeting rooms, and presentation facilities. Kauffman was the first residence hall to feature suite-style housing, which has become the norm for new residence halls at Nebraska.

## Coliseum

Ground was broken in 1925 for a new gymnasium facility, named the Coliseum on the suggestion of University business manager John Selleck, and the building was finished in time to hold the 1926 spring commencement ceremony. The University charged the Coliseum's construction costs against future gate receipts from Memorial Stadium, which opened in 1923. Designed by Ellery Davis, who also designed Memorial Stadium and Morrill Hall, the Coliseum includes ten large columns flanking the south-facing entry. The arched interior features a large floor suitable for basketball and a stage on the building's north end. During the 1930s, 1940s, and 1950s the Coliseum was the preferred location for dances—including performances by Glenn Miller and Tommy Dorsey—and hosted commencement ceremonies until the Devaney Center opened in 1976. The Coliseum was the home of the Husker volleyball team until 2013. Today it is part of the Campus Recreation center.

COLISEUM

## Robert Hillestad Textiles Gallery

Since 1997 a gallery in the Home Economics building on East Campus has borne the name Robert Hillestad Textiles Gallery, to honor an internationally known fiber artist and professor emeritus of textiles, merchandising, and fashion design. The gallery celebrates art, craft, design, and material culture through textiles and apparel exhibitions. Shows have included apparel from couture collections, experimental clothing, and student-created designs.

## Jackie Gaughan Multicultural Center

The Jackie Gaughan Multicultural Center, linked to the east side of the Nebraska Union, opened in 2010 after students voted in 2006 to assess a fee to fund a new center purpose-built for multicultural activities. The center features 30,000 square feet of space, including student offices, tutoring rooms, meeting rooms, and areas for faculty, staff, and students who are dedicated to diversity and multicultural programming. The center also houses the Kawasaki Reading Room, a center for Japanese studies at Nebraska, and various academic support programs. The center is named for Jackie D. Gaughan, who grew up in Nebraska but moved to Nevada, where he made his fortune in the hotel and casino industries. Jackie Gaughan was known as one of the first employers in Las Vegas to encourage minority hiring in a wide array of careers in the gaming industry. A major gift from the Gaughan family made the construction of the center possible.

## Native American Memorial and NAGPRA

The Native American Graves Protection and Repatriation Act (NAGPRA) became federal law in 1990. It requires universities receiving federal funding to inventory and repatriate to tribes all historic museum collections of Native American human remains. NAGPRA compliance at the University of Nebraska began with the October 3, 1991, repatriation of remains and funerary objects to the Omaha Tribe and the completion of the NAGPRA inventory in 1993. In 1998 human remains that had been overlooked during the federal inventory were discovered in Bessey Hall and other locations on campus. Tribes also alleged that faculty had conducted research on Omaha Tribal remains without proper tribal authorization. In addition, in August 1998 it was learned that sometime between 1965 and 1967 unidentified human remains from the anthropology teaching collection were burned in an incinerator formerly located north of the current East Campus Union.

Native American students, tribal members, and many others were deeply offended and outraged by these revelations. The University responded by convening and funding major NAGPRA meetings of sixteen Great Plains tribes starting in September 1998. As part of the reconciliation, the University adopted a moratorium on research on Native American remains and pledged to repatriate all Native American remains, even those classified as not known to be affiliated with a specific tribe. Chancellor James Moeser formally apologized to the tribes, and a memorial, dedicated in 2001, was placed at the location on East Campus where the incineration occurred.

Since 1991 UNL has repatriated the remains of over two thousand Native Americans. NAGPRA ensures that the human remains of Native people are treated with respect and dignity and that decisions regarding their disposition, further study, or reburial are made by Native American tribes.

# Legends and Legacies

## NEBRASKA ALUMNI AND NOTABLES

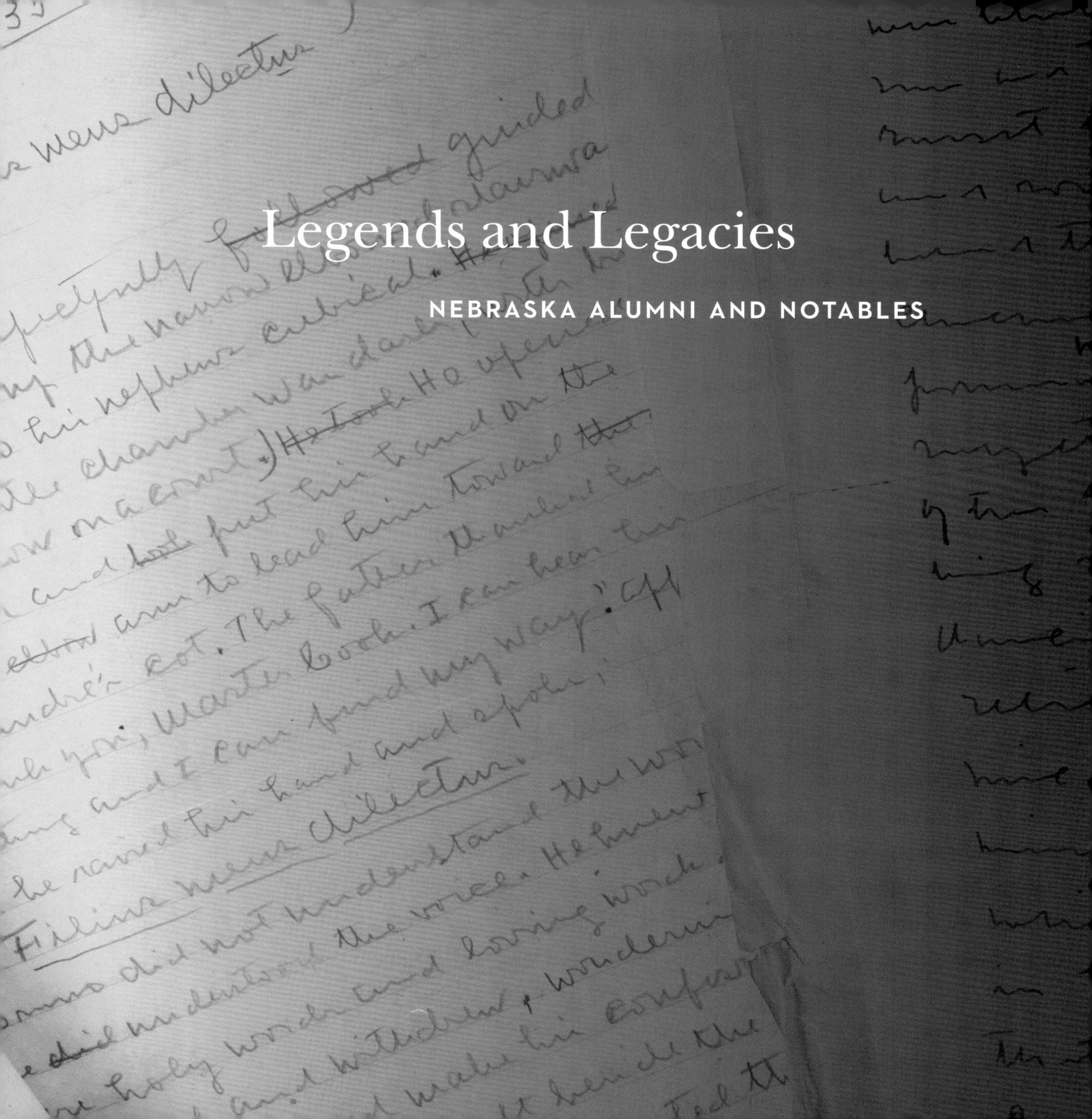

In the spring of 1873 William H. Shell and James Stuart Dales became the first graduates of the University of Nebraska. Since then Nebraska has conferred degrees on nearly 290,000 proud Husker students. The achievements of Nebraska alumni in their chosen fields—arts, humanities, technology, agriculture, politics, medicine, architecture, business, education, journalism—could fill volumes. Every day, Husker alumni make an impact in the world, from rural Nebraska farms to the streets of cities from coast to coast and distant locations around the globe. Every Nebraska alum writes a new story, adding to the vast array of alumni stories that have preceded them.

Nebraska's pantheon of alumni includes giants of business like Warren Buffett; statesmen such as Clayton Yeutter and Ted Sorensen; well-known entertainers like Johnny Carson (pictured at left; Carson's Carnac the Magnificent hat is on opposite page); revered authors and activists such as Willa Cather, Roxane Gay, and Grace and Edith Abbott; renowned artists like Aaron Douglas; and scientist-researchers such as George Beadle and Harold Edgerton. As students move into new fields of study—such as emerging digital media arts and innovative technologies that inform decisions about agriculture or marketing, improve teaching and learning in rural schools, or help heal brains damaged by concussion—or break new ground in traditional fields—such as finding ways to improve crop yields and nutritional content or understanding history and literature from the perspectives of marginalized people—Nebraska graduates will make their mark on society. This is the Nebraska difference.

## GRACE ABBOTT (1878–1939) AND EDITH ABBOTT (1876–1957)

Grace Abbott and Edith Abbott were two extraordinary sisters whose activism focused on children and immigrants, education reform, and elevating the profession of social work. Grace took graduate classes at Nebraska starting in about 1902, during summer vacations from teaching positions in her hometown of Grand Island, Nebraska. In 1907 she moved to Chicago's Hull House and earned a degree from the University of Chicago in political science. She focused on labor law reform and created the Immigrants' Protective League to protect immigrants from exploitation and help them integrate into American life. Grace was an early proponent of using sociological data, statistics, and research to aid in drafting laws and setting policy. In 1921 President Warren Harding appointed her head of the federal Children's Bureau. She helped draft the Social Security Act (with her sister, Edith) and worked for the new Social Security Administration from 1934–1939. Although not confirmed, Grace was the first woman to be nominated to a cabinet position. In 1931 *Good Housekeeping* magazine named her the fifth most influential woman alive. She held a professorship at the University of Chicago until her death in 1939. Grace is enshrined in the Nebraska Hall of Fame.

Edith worked on advancing the rights of immigrants, women, and children, and worked especially to end child labor. Although she began her career teaching, she took night courses and correspondence classes and earned an undergraduate degree from Nebraska in 1901. She won a fellowship to the University of Chicago, where she earned a doctorate in political economy in 1905. Edith focused on injecting humanitarian values into programs that sought to eliminate poverty rather than relying on punitive and judgmental "poor laws" that she believed stripped people of dignity. With a colleague Edith elevated Chicago's School of Social Work to a graduate-level program and in 1924 became the first female college dean in the United States. She reformed social work as a profession by emphasizing the need for education, for field experience working with clients, and for applying social statistics to study the root causes of poverty and find ways to alleviate it.

Edith and Grace lived together until Grace's death in 1939. Edith retired in 1942 and returned to Grand Island, where she lived until her death in 1957.

## HARTLEY BURR ALEXANDER (1873–1939)

A professor of philosophy at Nebraska, Hartley Burr Alexander is known for developing the iconography—the program of art and themes—for a number of monumental buildings, including the Nebraska State Capitol, Memorial Stadium, the Los Angeles Public Library, and Rockefeller Center in New York City. The son of a Methodist minister, Alexander grew up near Syracuse, Nebraska, then earned his bachelor's degree from Nebraska in 1897 and a doctorate from Columbia University in 1901. He worked as an editor in New York before joining the Nebraska faculty in 1908. Alexander was a poet and anthropologist and taught at Nebraska until 1928, when he left for Scripps College in Claremont, California, where he remained until his death. He also served as president of the American Philosophical Society.

## BION J. ARNOLD (1861–1942)

Considered the father of the "third rail" system that powers mass transit trains, Bion J. Arnold was a pioneer in electrical engineering who helped design New York's subway system. In 1893 he designed and built the elevated railway for Chicago's Columbian Exposition, before earning his graduate degree from the University of Nebraska in 1897. He assisted in the development of rapid transit trains into Grand Central Terminal in New York between 1898 and 1912, and when the line proved far more popular than predicted, he developed automatic speed control signal devices that allowed more trains to run during each hour. He also helped cities like Los Angeles and Pittsburgh convert to electrified railroads and developed cable car systems in San Francisco. Arnold was president of the American Institute of Electrical Engineers in 1903–1904, and during World War I he helped develop aerial torpedoes.

## HENRY M. BEACHELL (1906–2006)

Henry Beachell is credited with developing hybrid rice cultivars that improved yields and have fed the world. A 1930 graduate of Nebraska with a degree in agronomy, Beachell earned a master's degree from Kansas State University and joined the U.S. Department of Agriculture. The nine rice varieties he created account for more than 90 percent of U.S. long-grain rice production. In 1987 he was awarded the Japan Prize, which recognizes those who advance science, knowledge, and contribute to world peace and human prosperity, and in 1996 he received the World Food Prize (with his collaborator, Gurdev Khush). Beachell continued consulting with rice breeders until his death. Using the proceeds from his World Food Prize he established scholarships at Nebraska, Kansas State University, and Texas A&M University.

## BROOK BERRINGER (1973–1996)

Brook Berringer played at the quarterback position for the University of Nebraska football team from 1992 to 1995, and died tragically in a private plane crash on April 18, 1996. A memorial service was held at Memorial Stadium before the start of the 1996 Red-White spring game, with nearly fifty thousand in attendance. The University honors Berringer by awarding the Brook Berringer Memorial Scholarship to one football player each season who demonstrates outstanding integrity and character and by selecting players dedicated to volunteer work for the Brook Berringer Citizenship Team.

## CHARLES E. BESSEY (1845–1915)

Few individuals have had a greater impact on the University of Nebraska than Charles E. Bessey. Born in Ohio and educated at Michigan State University, Bessey came to Nebraska in 1884 with a vision for students to learn by observation and experimentation. He replaced a curriculum then heavy on library reading, lectures, and recitations with lab and field studies. He reportedly said, "Botany is the study of plants, not books." Acclaimed for his devotion to his students, Bessey taught more than four thousand of them over a forty-five-year career, many hundreds of whom made significant contributions to the sciences. Bessey's students developed the disciplines of plains ecology and range management and advanced the fields of agronomy, plant genetics, and crop physiology.

Bessey was also a formidable scientist in his own right. He devised a classification system for plants that is still in use; he published more than 150 papers; he wrote two botany textbooks, one of which was the most widely used in the field for a generation; and he edited two leading journals, *American Naturalist* and *Science*. His experiments in tree planting led to the eventual development of the Nebraska National Forest near Halsey, the first artificially planted national forest in the world, and he influenced legislation that legally protected California's sequoia trees. Bessey thrice served as interim or acting chancellor at Nebraska and he never retired; he died at age seventy in his home at 15th and R Streets, with publications still in progress. Nebraska's Bessey Hall was completed after his death, but the layout, with labs benefiting from natural light, was designed by Bessey.

In 2009 Charles Bessey was named to the Nebraska Hall of Fame, but his critical gift to the University of Nebraska was to instill the idea that scientists and scholars can make major disciplinary contributions with national and international implications while still focusing on teaching and issues of importance to the campus and state.

### LAWRENCE BRUNER (1856–1937)

Lawrence Bruner joined the Nebraska faculty in 1888, where he contributed to the sciences of both entomology and ornithology. Bruner was considered a world authority on grasshoppers and related insects, he founded the Nebraska Ornithological Union, he served as Nebraska's State Entomologist, he pioneered the discipline of economic entomology, and he led expeditions worldwide to collect and study insects and other specimens.

Bruner was born in Pennsylvania, but his family relocated to Nebraska when he was still an infant. When Bruner was fifteen he entered the University, although he never completed his degree. After observing the locust plagues of the early 1870s, he began serious study of grasshoppers, and by 1880 he was named to the U.S. Entomological Commission and later the USDA Division of Entomology. His arrival at Nebraska coincided with the first formal courses in entomology, and he was part of Bessey's famous Seminar Botanical group. In 1895 the Department of Entomology and Ornithology was created with Bruner as its faculty of one, and in 1897 the University conferred an honorary bachelor of science degree on Bruner, which is believed to be the only honorary bachelor of science degree ever awarded by the University.

### SUSAN ALICE BUFFETT (1953–PRESENT)

Susie Buffett, daughter of Warren Buffett, is one of Nebraska's leading philanthropists. She chairs the Sherwood Foundation and the Buffett Early Childhood Fund. The Buffett Early Childhood Fund works to improve early childhood education for young children growing up in low-income families, seeking to transform the early life experiences of children from birth through age eight. The fund supports the University of Nebraska system-wide Buffett Early Childhood Institute, which was created in 2011. Buffett also serves on several local and national nonprofit boards, including ONE, Girls Incorporated, and the Omaha Airport Authority.

### WARREN BUFFETT (1930–PRESENT)

Investor, businessman, and philanthropist Warren Buffett, the "Oracle of Omaha," is a 1950 graduate of Nebraska with a degree in business administration. Since then he has amassed a fortune—reportedly being the third-wealthiest person in America—while living and working in Omaha. As CEO of Berkshire Hathaway, Buffett has become the leading practitioner of "value investing," which involves buying stocks at less than their intrinsic value. Buffett has pledged to give the majority of his fortune to philanthropic causes, primarily through the Bill and Melinda Gates Foundation. Nebraska conferred an honorary degree on Warren Buffett in 1989.

## JOHNNY CARSON (1925–2005)

Johnny Carson was the longtime host of NBC's *The Tonight Show* from 1962 to 1992, during which time he perfected the late-night talk show genre into an art form. Carson won six Emmy Awards, a Peabody Award, and the Presidential Medal of Freedom. He also received a Kennedy Center Honor in 1993, where the Cornhusker Marching Band paid tribute to him and his Nebraska roots by playing "There Is No Place like Nebraska" and the "Tonight Show Theme" in his honor. The surprise appearance by the band visibly moved Carson.

Carson served as an ensign in the U.S. Navy during World War II before enrolling at the University of Nebraska in 1947, earning in 1949 a bachelor of arts in radio and speech with a minor in physics. Even before his death in 2005 Carson was generous to the University; his gifts benefited the Lied Center for Performing Arts, the Temple Building, and the Carson Center for Emerging Media Arts. Since 2011 more than $2 million from the Johnny Carson Foundation has supported the Johnny Carson Opportunity Scholarship fund for Nebraska high school graduates in the Hixson-Lied College of Fine and Performing Arts.

## WILLA CATHER (1873–1947)

Willa Cather continues to have a profound influence on the University. Born in Virginia, she was nine when her family moved to Nebraska. The move to the prairie, with its harsh weather, sense of isolation, and immigrant populations, deeply affected her and provided the initial imaginative materials for her richly successful career as journalist, editor, and, above all, fiction writer.

At UNL Cather edited the student newspaper, *The Hesperian*. She graduated in 1895 and launched a career in journalism that took her to Pittsburgh and on to New York, where she became managing editor for *McClure's*, one of the era's great magazines. In 1913 she published *O Pioneers!*, a novel set on the plains, followed by *The Song of the Lark* (1915) and *My Antonia* (1918). Cather became both a major Nebraska novelist and a writer with national outreach, and she received the Pulitzer Prize for Literature in 1923 for *One of Ours*. Her novels established Cather as a central figure in American letters. After her death, UNL figures such as Bernice Slote (Willa Cather scholar and editor of *Prairie Schooner*) and Virginia Faulkner (editor at the University of Nebraska Press) kept the Cather flame burning. Her works were included in the Nebraska English curriculum developed at the University for use by Nebraska public schools.

In 2001 Nebraska inaugurated the Willa Cather professorship to recognize faculty with the rank of full professor who have established exceptional records of distinguished scholarship or creative activity. During the State of Nebraska's Sesquicentennial in 2017, Cather was chosen as the most influential Nebraskan in state history by the *Lincoln Journal Star* newspaper. In 2018 the Nebraska Legislature voted to place Cather and Standing Bear in the U.S. Congress National Statuary Hall, replacing William Jennings Bryan and J. Sterling Morton.

## EDITH SCHWARTZ CLEMENTS (1874–1971) AND FREDERIC EDWARD CLEMENTS (1874–1945)

Frederic Clements entered the University of Nebraska at age sixteen; he earned a bachelor's degree in 1894, a master's degree in 1896, and a doctorate in 1898. He was a classmate of Roscoe Pound and Willa Cather and a member of Sem. Bot. Edith Schwartz earned a bachelor's degree in German in 1898 and was the first woman to earn a doctoral degree from Nebraska in 1904. Also a member of Sem. Bot., she was an athlete, an artist, and a scholar. Frederic and Edith were married in 1899.

Both Clementses were proteges of Charles Bessey, and Frederic taught botany at Nebraska from 1897 to 1907, eventually leaving to head the Botany Department at the University of Minnesota. At the same time, Edith taught German at Nebraska. Frederic eventually left academe and received funding from the Carnegie Institution of Washington, founding its Alpine Laboratory at Pike's Peak, Colorado. Edith and Frederic conducted research at Alpine as well as in Tucson, Arizona, and Santa Barbara, California, and they copublished extensively. Edith managed the laboratories, taught ecology, painted, and published guidebooks.

Frederic developed the "climax theory" of vegetation succession, which dominated the science of plant ecology during the twentieth century. The theory posits that vegetation communities move toward climax and stable states based on factors like climate, environment, and plant species. During Frederic's final years, he and Edith traveled and lectured to develop strategies to prevent a second Dust Bowl, establishing the foundations of the discipline of range management. Edith continued to write after Frederic's death.

## GRACE ELIZABETH CLEMENTS (1918–1965)

Grace Elizabeth "Betty" Clements (below, second from left) attended Nebraska on a Regents Scholarship, graduating in 1939 with a teaching degree. She became supervisor of girls' physical education at McCook, Nebraska, Public Schools and at McCook Junior College, and in 1941 she moved to Hastings, Nebraska, to supervise in the town's public schools and teach at Hastings College. She earned a pilot's license in 1942, joined the Army Air Corps Flight Training program, and was commissioned as a WASP. She later served in the Philippines in a medical unit. After World War II she entered the University of Nebraska College of Medicine and earned her MD in 1952. She was a neurologist in Phoenix and was a founding member of the Barrow Neurological Institute of St. Joseph's Hospital; she also was a consultant with the Veterans Administration Hospital. She posthumously received the Congressional Gold Medal in 2010, with other female World War II pilots.

## BEVERLY DEEPE KEEVER (1935–PRESENT)

The first woman war correspondent during the Vietnam War, Beverly Deepe Keever arrived in Vietnam in 1962 during what she had planned to be a brief stop during a world tour. She stayed in Vietnam seven years, working as a freelance journalist and developing sources and institutional knowledge that was the envy of others. She was the longest-serving American correspondent in Vietnam and her reporting was nominated for the Pulitzer Prize in 1969. Her book *Death Zones and Darling Spies: Seven Years of Vietnam War Reporting*, published in 2013 by the University of Nebraska Press, is a memoir of her experiences. Her personal archives reside with the University of Nebraska–Lincoln Libraries. She graduated from Nebraska in 1957, a Phi Beta Kappa and Mortar Board member, with dual majors in journalism and political science, and she received a master's degree from Columbia's School of Journalism before leaving for Vietnam. She taught journalism for twenty-nine years at the University of Hawaii, from which she earned both master's and doctoral degrees. She is a member of the Nebraska Women Journalists Hall of Fame.

## AARON DOUGLAS (1899–1979)

One of the most prominent artists of the Harlem Renaissance, Aaron Douglas graduated from the University of Nebraska in 1922 with a degree in fine arts, the first African American to do so. After relocating to Harlem, New York City, he worked with activists like W. E. B. DuBois and was an illustrator for magazines published by the NAACP and the Urban League. Douglas used his murals to depict the lives and history of African Americans. His style pioneered the use of traditional African motifs with modern aesthetics to explore themes of racism, segregation, and modern society. Douglas's art captures the zeitgeist of his era, and it helped establish a new black aesthetic. Douglas eventually moved to Nashville, where he founded the Art Department at Fisk University. He was affiliated with Fisk from 1937 to 1966. His works are held by leading museums, including Nebraska's Sheldon Museum of Art. The University of Nebraska honors Douglas by awarding a professorship that recognizes full professors who demonstrate extraordinary teaching excellence and national visibility for instructional practice.

## HAROLD "DOC" EDGERTON (1903–1990)

A native Nebraskan, Harold Edgerton earned a bachelor's in electrical engineering from Nebraska in 1925 and master's and doctoral degrees from the Massachusetts Institute of Technology. A colleague inspired him to use a strobe light in photography to make moving objects appear to slow down. In 1937 he teamed with photographer Gjon Mili in using multiple flash units and the stroboscope to create art. The strobe flashed up to 120 times per second, making the camera appear to freeze movement. The strikingly beautiful images have become popular and they hang in museums worldwide. A short film he made using the technique won an Oscar in 1940.

During World War II Edgerton and his colleagues developed a camera to be used in aerial nighttime photography, and after the war the Atomic Energy Commission asked Edgerton to photograph nuclear explosions. His deep-sea photography devices as well as his sonar technology have been used to search for shipwrecks, ancient cities, and geologic anomalies and to understand ocean life.

### LOREN EISELEY (1907–1977)

Born and raised in Lincoln, Loren Eiseley earned a bachelor of art degree in English and a bachelor of science degree in geology and anthropology from Nebraska in 1933. While at Nebraska he served as editor of *Prairie Schooner* and participated in archaeological digs led by the State Museum. After earning a doctorate in 1937 from the University of Pennsylvania, he taught at the University of Kansas, then at Oberlin before returning to Penn in 1947. At his death Eiseley was Benjamin Franklin Professor of Anthropology and History of Science there.

Eiseley wrote more than a dozen books, and he is most widely known for his personal essays at the intersection of humanism and science. His writing about human origins and the relationship between humans and the natural world brought him legions of fans in an era of introspection and interest in the natural environment. After his death a collection of his notebooks, thought to have been destroyed, were published. He is enshrined in the State of Nebraska's Hall of Fame with a bust in the State Capitol. A public library in Lincoln also bears Eiseley's name.

### JAY WRIGHT FORRESTER (1918–2016)

Jay Wright Forrester developed magnetic memory methods for computers, and he is credited with creating the first computer animation—a jumping ball on an oscilloscope. A native of Anselmo, Nebraska, Forrester earned a degree from Nebraska in 1939. In 1956 Forrester transferred to MIT's new Sloan School of Management. He is known as the founder of "system dynamics," a discipline that examines business, economic, environmental, and social systems by using simulations that can predict and detect problems arising in complex networks. In 1961 Forrester published *Industrial Dynamics*, a breakthrough in the field of management that describes how minor changes in a system can have catastrophic or advantageous consequences. He invented the "Beer Game," which is used to examine supply chain management and challenge students to question their own beliefs rather than using only data to drive decisions.

### ROXANE GAY (1974–PRESENT)

A contemporary author, feminist, and professor, Roxane Gay is a Haitian American who grew up in Omaha. She earned her master's degree in creative writing from Nebraska in 2004. She is the author of many works, including the best-selling essay collection *Bad Feminist* (2014), the short story collection *Difficult Women* (2017), and the memoir *Hunger* (2017). Much of her work focuses on feminist sexual identity and racial issues viewed through her personal lived experience as a non-cis black woman of size. She is a rape survivor and talks openly of how that experience has shaped her life. An associate professor of English at Purdue University, she also contributes opinion essays to a number of publications, including the *New York Times*.

## BARBARA HENDRICKS (1948–PRESENT)

Musician and humanitarian Barbara Hendricks graduated from the University of Nebraska at age twenty with dual majors in chemistry and mathematics. She then entered the Aspen Music Festival and School and the Juilliard School, where she studied with the opera great Maria Callas. She made her opera debut in 1974 and has performed on the world's most prominent stages, including the Metropolitan Opera, the Paris Opera, and the Royal Opera House in London. She also performs a jazz repertoire and has made numerous recordings and films. Now a Swedish citizen, Hendricks has devoted much of her life to humanitarian causes, particularly ones focused on the plight of refugees. She is a longtime supporter of the United Nations High Commissioner for Refugees (UNHCR) and was named an UNHCR Goodwill Ambassador in 1987 and an Honorary Lifetime Goodwill Ambassador in 2002. In 1998 she founded the Barbara Hendricks Foundation for Peace and Reconciliation, which seeks to facilitate reconciliation where conflicts have occurred. In 2001 she performed at the Nobel Prize ceremony in Oslo at the invitation of Kofi Annan. Nebraska conferred an honorary degree on Hendricks in 2015.

## GLADYS ROWENA HENRY DICK (1881–1963)

A physician, Gladys Henry Dick codeveloped a vaccine for scarlet fever. A 1900 graduate of Nebraska with a degree in zoology, Gladys Henry took graduate classes at Nebraska until 1903, when she enrolled in Johns Hopkins University School of Medicine, earning her medical degree in 1907. She then studied in Berlin and became interested in biomedical research. After moving to Chicago, where she contracted scarlet fever, she began studying the disease's effect on the kidneys. In 1914 she married a co-researcher from the University of Chicago, George Dick. In 1923 they discovered scarlet fever was caused by streptococcus bacteria and they developed a skin test to determine a patient's susceptibility to the disease. They created a vaccine for treatment and prevention and were nominated for the Nobel Prize in 1925.

## LETA STETTER HOLLINGWORTH (1886–1939)

Leta Stetter Hollingworth, a 1906 Nebraska graduate, was a pioneer in the fields of the psychology of women, clinical psychology, and educational psychology. Known for her work with children, she also coined the term "gifted" in describing children of high intelligence. While at Nebraska she contributed to the *Daily Nebraskan*, the *Sombrero*, and the *Senior Book*. Leta graduated Phi Beta Kappa and took teaching jobs in small towns in Nebraska. In 1908 she married Harry Hollingworth and moved to New York. Because New York prohibited married women from teaching, she turned her attention to sociology, focusing on women's social roles and inequality. She received master's and doctoral degrees from Columbia University, and her dissertation refuted then-prevailing theories that women's menstrual cycles caused mental incapacities. She also challenged the idea that women were intellectually inferior to men, arguing that cultural practices that limited women's occupations and roles constrained women's capacities and talents. She wrote a number of influential books on child psychology, teaching, and parenting.

### ALVIN SAUNDERS JOHNSON (1874–1971)

Born near Homer, Nebraska, Alvin Johnson graduated from the University in 1897 with a degree in classics. He earned his PhD in economics from Columbia and taught at a number of prestigious institutions, including Bryn Mawr, Columbia, Cornell, Nebraska, Stanford, and Texas. In 1922 he became director and later president of the New School for Social Research, a progressive institution in New York City founded in 1919 to challenge traditional ways of thinking. In the 1930s the University-in-Exile at the New School, established by Johnson, provided safety to many Jewish scholars endangered by Nazi persecution. He was additionally instrumental in developing legislation banning discrimination in employment and education. In 2014 Johnson was inducted into the State of Nebraska Hall of Fame.

### HIRAM HISANORI KANO (1889–1988)

Born in Japan, Hiram Hisanori Kano came to Nebraska in 1916 at the urging of William Jennings Bryan. Kano earned a master's degree in agricultural economics in 1918 and later worked for Nebraska Extension. A devoted Christian and baptized at age twenty in Japan, Kano began serving the seven hundred or so Japanese Americans living in western Nebraska, first as a lay pastor in the Episcopal Church and later as an ordained minister serving congregations in Mitchell and North Platte. The FBI arrested Kano in North Platte the day on Pearl Harbor was attacked; he was the only Nebraskan incarcerated during the war. In 2015 the Episcopal Church added Kano to its official church calendar, which recognizes the work of holy people and is the equivalent of sainthood. His day of remembrance is October 24.

### BOB KERREY (1943–PRESENT)

J. Robert "Bob" Kerrey was born and raised in Lincoln, Nebraska, and earned his pharmacy degree from Nebraska in 1966. He served as a U.S. Navy SEAL officer in Vietnam and was awarded the Congressional Medal of Honor in 1970. Kerrey served one term as governor of Nebraska from 1983 to 1987. He was elected senator in 1988, reelected in 1994, and served until January 2001. He was president of the New School in New York City from 2001 to 2010, during which time the school grew in enrollment and more than doubled its endowment. Kerrey also served on the National Commission on Terrorist Attacks Upon the United States.

## ROBERT E. KNOLL (1922–2009)

Known for his exemplary teaching, especially his undergraduate classes on Shakespeare, English professor Robert E. Knoll retired in 1990 as the D. B. and Paula Varner Professor of English. After retirement he began what became his final book, *Prairie University: A History of the University of Nebraska,* published in 1995 by the University of Nebraska Press. The witty and opinionated book reveals his voice on every page. Knoll graduated from Nebraska in 1943 and joined the English Department in 1950. In the interim he had earned a PhD from Minnesota and served with the U.S. Army in the Philippines and later with the Occupation Army in Japan.

A scholar of Renaissance literature, Knoll wrote on Shakespeare's contemporaries Ben Jonson and Christopher Marlowe and Midwestern regional writers Robert McAlmon, Weldon Kees, and Wright Morris. He was a founding faculty member and director of Nebraska's Centennial Education Program in 1969, a Woods Fellow at the Warburg Institute in London, a Fulbright Professor in Austria, and a National Humanities Institute Fellow at Yale. After his death, the University created the Robert E. Knoll Lecture Series, and in 2010 the Robert E. Knoll Residential Center opened on City Campus.

## BEN KUROKI (1917–2015)

Born in Gothenburg, Nebraska, and raised in Hershey, Ben Kuroki was the only Japanese-American gunner in the Army Air Forces of World War II. He flew fifty-eight raids and earned three Distinguished Flying Crosses for service over North Africa, Europe, and Japan. After the war he became a journalist. Kuroki received the Distinguished Service Medal in 2005, during which time the University of Nebraska conferred an honorary degree to complement the bachelor's degree he had earned from Nebraska in 1950. NET television's 2007 documentary, *Most Honorable Son,* highlights his war experiences.

## RACHEL LLOYD (1839–1900)

Rachel Holloway Lloyd became the first woman to earn a doctoral degree from the University of Zurich in 1887. (Women were not allowed to earn doctoral degrees in the United States until 1890.) Lloyd received a certificate in chemistry from Harvard University after which she headed a pharmacy school. In 1881 she was the first American woman to publish in a major American chemistry journal. Her analysis of sugar concentration in sugar beets and how to improve beet varieties promoted an important agricultural commodity for the state of Nebraska. She joined the Nebraska faculty in 1887 as the second member of the Chemistry Department and the only one to hold a doctorate. Lloyd founded a number of societies and clubs in Lincoln, including the Nebraska Academy of Sciences, the Nebraska Local Section of the American Chemical Society, and the Haydon Art Club of the University of Nebraska, which was the precursor of the Nebraska Art Association and is now the Sheldon Art Association.

## PATSY MATSU TAKEMOTO MINK (1927–2002)

Japanese American Patsy Takemoto Mink was the first Asian American and woman of color elected to Congress and is noted for coauthoring the Title IX Amendment of the Higher Education Act, which prohibits gender discrimination by federally funded institutions. Mink enrolled at Nebraska in 1947. After experiencing the University's racial segregation policies in residence halls, she organized a coalition of students, parents, administrators, faculty, staff, alumni, and businesses to protest this segregation. Elected as president of the Unaffiliated Students of the University of Nebraska, a separate student government for nonwhite students, Mink and her coalition successfully lobbied to end the University's discriminatory housing policy.

After completing her degree in premedicine at Nebraska and being rejected from more than twenty schools because they refused to accept a woman, she instead earned a law degree from the University of Chicago in 1951. She was the first Japanese-American woman to practice law in Hawaii. An active Democrat, she served in Hawaii's territorial and later state legislatures. In 1965 Mink was elected to the U.S. Congress, serving six consecutive terms. She left Congress to serve as assistant secretary of state in the Carter administration. She returned to Congress in 1990, serving six additional terms before her death in 2002.

## DIRK OBBINK (1957–PRESENT)

Dirk Obbink's work in recovering texts from ancient carbonized papyrus scrolls earned him a MacArthur Genius Award in 2001. A papyrologist and classics scholar, Obbink has expertise in the science of rescuing manuscripts using multispectral photography, carbon dating, and imaging techniques. Obbink earned his bachelor's and master's degrees in classics from Nebraska in 1979 and 1984; he earned his doctorate from Stanford. He is a lecturer in papyrology and Greek literature in the Faculty of Classics at Oxford University and is the head of the Oxyrhynchus Papyri Project. Obbink is also a fellow and tutor in the University of Oxford (Christ Church). In 2014 he attributed two lines of poetry found on an Egyptian mummy casing to the poet Sappho, born around 620 BCE and considered one of history's most influential poets.

## JOHN J. PERSHING (1860–1948)

In 1891 2nd Lieutenant John J. Pershing was assigned to Nebraska as a professor of military science and tactics. The next year Pershing organized a competition drill group, subsequently named the Pershing Rifles after Pershing left Nebraska, which has become a national military drill group. While at Nebraska, Pershing pursued and earned a law degree. In 1895 he was reassigned to Montana to lead the Tenth Cavalry's Buffalo Soldiers, an African-American unit, and six months later he was teaching at West Point. Pershing's distinguished military career sent him to the Philippines, Japan, Cuba, Mexico, and eventually Europe, where he was U.S. commander of the American Expeditionary Force during World War I. After retiring in 1924 Pershing published a two-volume memoir, which won a Pulitzer Prize in 1932.

## LOUISE POUND (1872–1958)

Lincoln native Louise Pound was a respected literary scholar, athlete, and musician. The younger sister of Roscoe Pound (a notable legal scholar and the dean of Nebraska's College of Law), Louise was determined to outshine him. As an undergraduate at Nebraska she was friends with Willa Cather and both were active in the University's literary societies. Pound earned a doctorate in Germany and was a professor of English at Nebraska for fifty years. A prolific scholar, Pound focused on American authors and folkways and was a pioneer in the linguistic study of American English, including pronunciation and word creation. She was the first woman president of the Modern Language Association.

As an undergraduate and throughout her life Pound was a natural athlete, excelling in golf, bicycling, basketball, rowing, and winning numerous titles in tennis competitions. She was a proud proponent of women's athletics throughout her life. Pound's namesake building, part of twin high-rise residence halls built on City Campus in 1963, was razed in December 2017. Her name now graces the former College of Business Administration building as Louise Pound Hall.

## MARI SANDOZ (1896–1966)

Mari Sandoz is one of Nebraska's most respected authors. Her biography of her father, *Old Jules* (1935), and works such as *Crazy Horse: Strange Man of the Oglalas* (1942) and *Cheyenne Autumn* (1953) won her international respect as a writer and chronicler of the settlement of the West and as a champion of Native Americans. Sandoz wrote more than twenty books and dozens of short stories and articles about the Great Plains. Born to Swiss immigrants on a northcentral Nebraska homestead, she endured a difficult childhood with a sometimes violent father. She enrolled at Nebraska in 1922 but did not earn a degree. She wrote prolifically, though she said that she received more than a thousand rejection letters and burned more than seventy of her manuscripts in frustration. Sandoz had to fight with publishers to retain vernacular Western language and slang and Native American idioms, cadences, and speech patterns in her works.

*Slogum House* (1937) and *Capital City* (1939) earned acclaim but also backlash from the books' perceived attacks on the character of Nebraskans, and Sandoz eventually moved to New York City, where she lived until her death. The University of Nebraska conferred an honorary degree on Sandoz in 1950 and a City Campus residence hall is named for her.

## ELLEN SMITH (1838–1903)

Ellen Smith was the first woman faculty member at the University of Nebraska. Smith was hired in 1877 as an instructor in Greek and Latin; she was also principal of the Latin School until she was named University registrar, a position she held from 1884 to 1902. In 1895 "Ma Smith," as she was often called, was named "Custodian of the Library" during its move from University Hall to the new library. Like many women of her day, Smith was treated poorly in terms of salary equity. She retired in 1902 after failed salary negotiations with the Board of Regents. She died six months later. In 1920 a home used by the dean of women for women's activities was renamed Ellen Smith Hall. In the 1950s the building was razed to make room for the current Canfield Administration Building. The current Ellen Smith Hall is part of the Harper-Schramm-Smith residence hall complex.

## THEODORE C. SORENSEN (1928–2010)

Theodore C. Sorensen graduated Phi Beta Kappa in 1949 from the University of Nebraska with a bachelor's degree in law, and in 1951 he earned his juris doctor from the University of Nebraska College of Law. Upon graduation, Sorensen worked as a researcher, advisor, counselor, and speechwriter for then Sen. John F. Kennedy. He purportedly helped write Kennedy's inaugural address, which includes the immortal line "Ask not what your country can do for you—ask what you can do for your country" and challenged Americans to greater good. In 1962 Sorensen drafted Kennedy's letter to Soviet leader Nikita Khrushchev, which helped end the Cuban Missile Crisis. After JFK's death in 1963 Sorensen joined a New York law firm as an international lawyer. He also wrote the bestselling biography *Kennedy* and advised Robert F. Kennedy during Kennedy's 1968 presidential campaign. In 1993 Sorensen received the Law College's Distinguished Alumnus Award and in 2008 established the Theodore C. Sorensen Public Service Scholarship for seniors in the College of Arts and Sciences who demonstrate superior academic performance and a commitment to public service.

## JAMES MEYERS THOMPSON (1906–1977)

A novelist and screenwriter, Jim Thompson attended Nebraska from 1929 to 1931 under a program for gifted writers from "untraditional educational backgrounds." He did not graduate. He headed Oklahoma's Federal Writers' Project efforts, working with Louis L'Amour, and eventually settled into the lucrative but less prestigious crime fiction genre. His most famous work, *The Killer Inside Me*, was published in 1952 and has twice been made into a movie. The acclaimed *Savage Night* followed in 1953, and he wrote ten more novels in the following two years. Thompson's 1963 novel *The Grifters* also was made into a film, as was *The Getaway* (1958). Thompson wrote more than thirty novels and worked as a screenwriter in Hollywood with Robert Redford, Robert Mitchum, Stanley Kubrick, and Sam Peckinpah.

## EVAN WILLIAMS (1972–PRESENT)

Evan Williams, with two other partners, cofounded Twitter, the social media company, in 2006. Williams, who grew up near Clarks, Nebraska, enrolled at Nebraska in 1990 and dropped out eighteen months later to start a company that designed websites for local businesses and made CD-ROMS about Nebraska football and the internet. Poor timing caused the company to fail. Williams moved to California, where he worked at a number of startups, including Blogger, an early internet blogging platform that eventually sold to Google. Williams co-founded Odeo, a podcast company, and created Medium, an online publishing platform. Williams spoke at spring commencement in 2017, when Nebraska granted him an honorary degree.

## CLAYTON K. YEUTTER (1930–2017)

Born in Eustis, Nebraska, Clayton Yeutter worked on his family farm before earning a B.S. in 1952, graduating first in his class. After serving five years in the U.S. Air Force, Yeutter returned to the University in 1960, where he worked as a faculty member in agricultural economics and earned a law degree cum laude in 1963 and a doctorate in agricultural economics in 1966.

Yeutter served as Nebraska governor Norbert Tiemann's chief of staff from 1966 to 1968 and CEO of the Chicago Mercantile Exchange from 1978 to 1984. He then became a U.S. trade representative for President Ronald Reagan. Yeutter's work in international trade laid the groundwork for the North American Free Trade Agreement. He was U.S. Secretary of Agriculture for President George H. W. Bush from 1989 to 1991 and was later Bush's chief domestic policy advisor. He also served as national chairman of the Republican Party.

Nebraska conferred an honorary degree upon Yeutter in 1988. In 2014 a statue of Yeutter was dedicated on East Campus, as part of a set of statues honoring Nebraskans who have served as U.S. Secretary of Agriculture. In 2015 a gift from Yeutter to the University created three endowed chairs and established the Clayton K. Yeutter Institute of International Trade and Finance at Nebraska to help students prepare to work in global economics.

# Nobel Prize Winners

Nebraska alumni **George Beadle**, **Donald Cram**, and **Alan Heeger** are all Nobel Prize winners. **George Beadle** (1903–1989) shared the 1958 Nobel Prize in Physiology or Medicine for his discovery, with co-recipient Edward Tatum, that genes determine the structure of enzymes and thereby affect heredity. Dubbed the "one gene–one enzyme" concept, Beadle and Tatum's work (undertaken at Stanford University) helped found the field of biochemical genetics.

A native of Wahoo, **George Beadle** earned a B.S. degree in agriculture from Nebraska in 1926 and a master's degree in 1927. At Nebraska he worked with Professor F. D. Keim, a protégé of the great botanist Charles Bessey, on wheat breeding; he earned his doctorate in 1931 from Cornell University. Beadle, a faculty member at several universities, was known for his enthusiasm and humor. Beadle became chancellor and then president of the University of Chicago, where he served until his retirement. Nebraska's Beadle Center, home to programs in biotechnology, biosciences, and plant sciences, is named in his honor. Nebraska awarded him an honorary Doctor of Science degree in 1949.

**Donald Cram** (1919–2001) shared the 1987 Nobel Prize in Chemistry with four other scientists for successfully building molecules able to "host" (attract and bind) other molecules. This "host-guest" work made a significant impact on the field of organic chemistry.

Cram earned a degree in chemistry from Rollins College in 1941. In 1942 he earned a master's degree in organic chemistry from Nebraska, and a doctorate in organic chemistry from Harvard in 1947. He became a faculty member at UCLA in 1947 and remained there for the entirety of his career, becoming well known by his students for playing guitar during class and as an avid surfer.

Cram's work allowed for development in the laboratory of functional enzymes that behave like natural enzymes. He discovered what has become known as "Cram's rule of asymmetric induction," which in part explains how molecules form. Nebraska awarded him an honorary degree in 1989.

**Alan Heeger** (1936–present) shared the 2000 Nobel Prize in Chemistry for his work in discovering and developing certain plastics that can conduct electricity. Heeger, born in Iowa, earned his bachelor's degree in physics and mathematics from Nebraska in 1957 and his doctorate in physics from the University of California, Berkeley, in 1961.

In his official Nobel biography, Heeger relates that he entered Nebraska to pursue engineering, not knowing that science could be a career path. After one semester he transferred to physics and mathematics, studying with Professor Theodore "Ted" Jorgensen, who introduced him to quantum physics and modern science. Of his time at Nebraska, Heeger said, "The combination of partying and intellectual awakening is what the undergraduate years are supposed to be." Nebraska conferred an honorary Doctor of Science degree on Heeger in 1999.

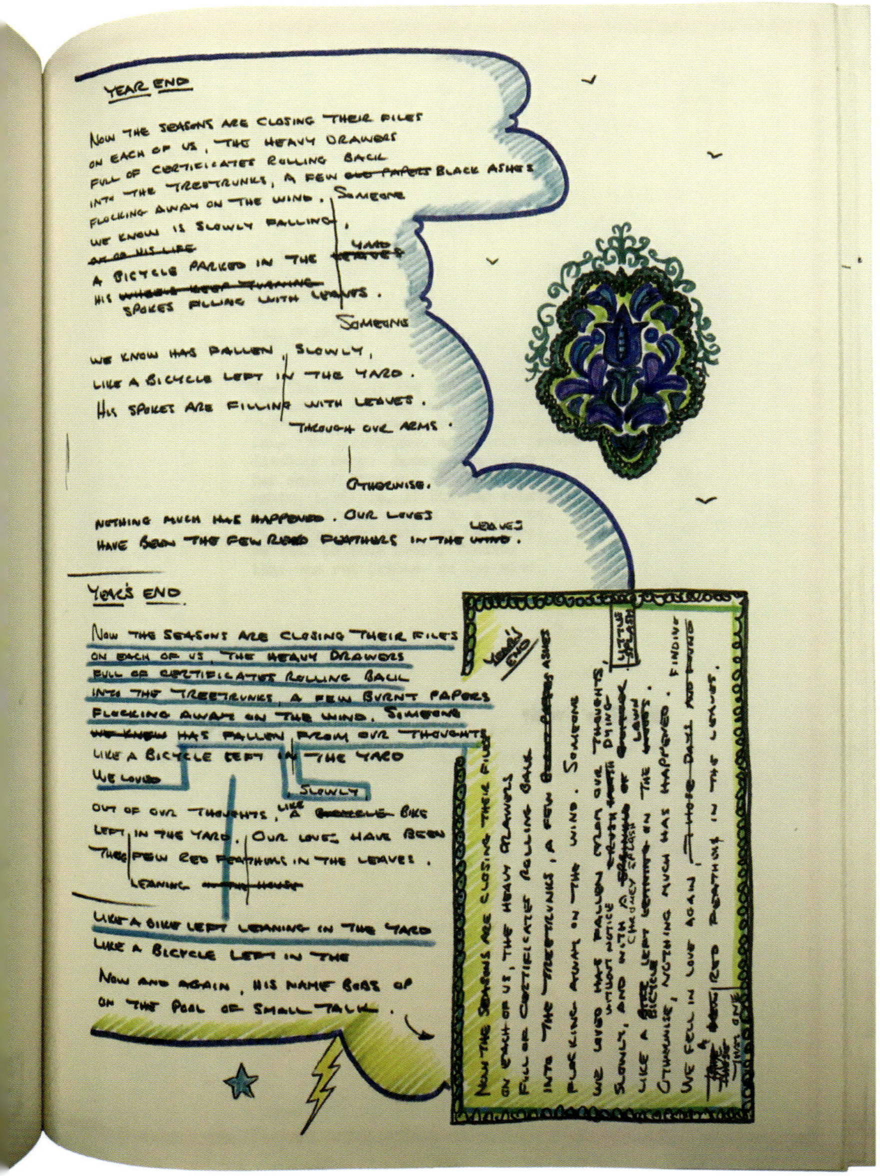

# Pulitzer Prize Winners

Nebraska alumni and faculty have won numerous Pulitzer Prizes since the prize was established in 1917. Pulitzer Prizes are awarded annually, recognizing outstanding accomplishments in journalism, letters, music, and drama.

## Faculty

**John J. Pershing, 1932**, History, for *My Experiences in the World War*. Pershing was a faculty member from 1891 to 1895. In his acceptance remarks Pershing mentioned Willa Cather, who won a Pulitzer Prize in 1922 and who was a mathematics student under Pershing.

**Karl Shapiro, 1945**, Poetry, for *V-Letter and Other Poems*. Shapiro was U.S. Poet Laureate in 1946–47. Shapiro later became a member of Nebraska's English faculty and editor of *Prairie Schooner* from 1956 to 1966.

**Ted Kooser, 2005**, Poetry, for *Delights and Shadows*. Kooser, who was U.S. Poet Laureate from 2004 to 2006, teaches poetry writing in the Department of English.

**Matt Waite, 2009**, National Reporting, for election coverage and development of the website PolitiFact, the first website ever awarded a Pulitzer. He is a professor of practice in journalism and a 1997 Nebraska graduate.

## Alumni

**Harvey Newbranch, 1920**, Editorial Writing, for an editorial in the Omaha *Evening World-Herald* titled "Law and the Jungle," which decried a lynching that occurred in Omaha. Newbranch was an 1896 graduate.

**Willa Cather, 1923**, Novel, *One of Ours*. Cather graduated from Nebraska in 1895.

**Robert Lasch, 1965**, Editorial Writing, *St. Louis Post-Dispatch*. Lasch, a Rhodes Scholar, graduated from Nebraska in 1928.

**James V. Risser, 1976**, National Reporting, for uncovering large-scale corruption in the grain export trade. **1979**, National Reporting, for a series on farming damage to the environment. The articles were published in the *Des Moines Register*. Risser earned a bachelor's degree in psychology at Nebraska and later a certificate in journalism in 1962, after completing law school in California.

**Charles Mohr, 1986**, Explanatory Journalism, for a six-part series on the Strategic Defense Initiative written by a team of five reporters and published in the *New York Times*. Mohr was a 1951 Nebraska graduate who was an early *Times* correspondent covering the Vietnam War.

**Karen Blessen, 1989**, Explanatory Reporting. Co-recipient for work on a special report on a 1985 plane crash, the follow-up investigation, and implications for air safety that was published by the *Dallas Morning News*. Blessen was the first newspaper graphic artist to win a Pulitzer. Blessen graduated from Nebraska in 1973.

**Marjie Lundstrom, 1991**, National Reporting. Co-recipient, with Gannett News Service, for reporting that disclosed that hundreds of child abuse-related deaths go undetected each year as a result of errors by medical examiners. Lundstrom is a 1978 Nebraska graduate.

**Jeff Zeleny, 2000**, Explanatory Reporting, for a team-reported series on air traffic control problems published by the *Chicago Tribune*. Now national correspondent for CNN, Zeleny is a 1996 Nebraska graduate.

**Christine Graves, 2018**, Local Reporting, for work with a sixty-member team that examined the impact of heroin in Ohio, published in the *Cincinnati Enquirer*. Graves, a 1987 Nebraska graduate, was a reporter/writer for the project.

**Nate Kelly, 2018**, Explanatory Reporting, for work with thirty journalists looking at the possible impact of building a border wall. Kelly was video content strategist and in charge of photojournalists on the project. He is a 2010 Nebraska graduate.

# University of Nebraska–Lincoln Chancellors

### RONNIE GREEN (2016–PRESENT)

Ronnie Green is the twentieth chancellor of the University of Nebraska–Lincoln. Prior to being named chancellor in May of 2016, Green served for six years as the Harlan Vice Chancellor of UNL's Institute of Agriculture and Natural Resources. In this role he also jointly served as the vice president for agriculture and natural resources of the University of Nebraska system. Green also served previously as UNL's senior vice chancellor for academic affairs.

### HARVEY PERLMAN (2000–2016)

Harvey Perlman served one of the longest and most consequential chancellorships in the history of the institution, and set the university on new trajectories for upward growth and prosperity. On his watch the University built major new facilities, opened Nebraska Innovation Campus, was a key partner in major urban renewal projects that transformed the city of Lincoln, and joined the nation's most prestigious academic and athletic organization, the Big Ten Conference.

### JAMES MOESER (1996–2000)

As chancellor, James Moeser strengthened undergraduate education by increasing the rigor of Nebraska's undergraduate curriculum while simultaneously improving the University's recruitment and retention of students. Moeser worked to build on Nebraska's strengths in research and graduate studies in order to meet the needs of Nebraska and the nation. He also promoted a campus culture that encouraged the growth and development of students' ethical and value systems. In addition, during Moeser's tenure the University received the three largest gifts ever given to the University of Nebraska.

### GRAHAM SPANIER (1994–1996)

When Graham Spanier arrived at Nebraska, the University was facing a $6 million budget cut, morale was low among faculty and staff, several high-level administrative positions were being filled on an interim basis, and overall admission standards were low. Over the next four years of his chancellorship, Spanier solved the budget crisis, revitalized the University's affirmative action office, and raised admissions standards, among other accomplishments.

### MARTIN A. MASSENGALE (1981–1994)

As chancellor Martin Massengale was known as an effective leader and supporter of integrating research, education, and extension. Among his many duties as chancellor, Massengale was responsible administratively for the Lied Center when it opened in 1990, and he oversaw the creation of the Center for Grassland Studies. Massengale is president emeritus of the University of Nebraska, director of the Center for Grassland Studies, and an NU Foundation distinguished professor.

### ROY YOUNG (1976–1980)

Upon his arrival in Lincoln from Oregon State University, Roy Young was charged with increasing research activity and outside funding. By 1980 the University had achieved a record $30 million in grants, contracts, and gifts—$8 million more than the previous year and $11 million more than the year before that. Young set up a system of faculty development fellowships similar to sabbaticals, and initiated the University's affiliation with the National Merit Scholars Program in 1978 in an effort to provide more opportunities for Merit Scholars to attend the University. Young also led efforts to increase quality standards for student admissions and enhance teaching and research programs.

## JAMES ZUMBERGE (1972–1975)

A renowned explorer of the Antarctic, James Zumberge became chancellor immediately following the reorganization of the University of Nebraska into one system, which included separating the medical center and moving the College of Pharmacy from Lincoln to Omaha. James Zumberge's most significant contribution as chancellor was the formation of UNL's Institute of Agriculture and Natural Resources.

## JOSEPH SOSHNIK (1968–1971)

Joseph Soshnik was the first and only "president" of the University of Nebraska–Lincoln. The University of Nebraska system came into being on July 1, 1968, and then-chancellor Clifford Hardin was made head of the entire NU system while Soshnik was named president of UNL. By the end of Soshnik's term the system had again been reorganized and the titles president and chancellor were switched.

## CLIFFORD M. HARDIN (1954–1968)

At the time of his appointment, Clifford Hardin was the youngest university president in the country at thirty-eight years old. Within his first month as chancellor, Hardin began the process of applying to the Michigan-based Kellogg Foundation for a national extension center. Hardin secured the funds, along with local matching grants, and the resulting Nebraska Center for Continuing Education was dedicated in 1961, renamed Hardin Hall in 1994. In 1962 Hardin hired Bob Devaney as football coach, beginning the modern era of Nebraska athletics. In 1968 Hardin left his position as chancellor to serve as U.S. Secretary of Agriculture in the incoming Nixon Administration.

## REUBEN G. GUSTAVSON (1946–1953)

World War II ended one year before Reuben Gustavson became chancellor, and veterans enrolling under the GI Bill resulted in a one-year doubling of UNL's enrollment (1945–46). Adjusting to the new size and demographics of the student body proved challenging, but Gustavson focused the University on new knowledge and research. He saw the administration and faculty as partners on the same mission and brought faculty into policy and strategic decision-making. A tireless advocate for equality, Gustavson led a successful effort to integrate the dormitories and enact nondiscriminatory policies throughout the University.

## CHAUNCEY SAMUEL BOUCHER (1938–1946)

Chauncey Boucher served the University in a period that included the end of the Great Depression and the start of World War II. A noted professor of American history before being hired as chancellor at Nebraska, Boucher instituted admission standards and faculty committees on educational policy, practice, and research. Boucher submitted his resignation in early 1945, as the tumult of a coming war descended on the country and the University.

## EDGAR A. BURNETT (1927–1938)

Edgar Burnett's years at the University as director of animal husbandry, dean of agriculture, and as chancellor—years that coincided with the end of the Roaring Twenties and the beginning of the Great Depression—were marked by some of its best and some of its worst times. The prolonged period of scarcity during which Burnett governed the University led him to recognize that the University could not rely on state funding alone. Always a practical man, Burnett responded to the situation with his most lasting contribution to the University: establishment of the University of Nebraska Foundation in 1936.

## SAMUEL AVERY (1908–1927)

Samuel Avery was a professor of agricultural chemistry at Nebraska when he was tapped to serve as interim chancellor in 1908, following the resignation of Elisha Benjamin Andrews. The "interim" was dropped from his title in December of that year when the Board of Regents officially elected him chancellor. Avery was "devoted to his university," and the school's talented faculty, including luminaries such as Louise Pound, Hartley Burr Alexander, and Charles E. Bessey, sustained Nebraska's reputation. Avery returned to his first loves, the chemistry lab and teaching, in 1927. Avery Laboratory (today's Avery Hall) was dedicated in his name in 1916.

## ELISHA BENJAMIN ANDREWS (1900–1908)

At the turn of the century Nebraska was a formidable institution of national stature, and it grew under Elisha Andrews's leadership. It was during Andrews's time that the University's athletic teams adopted a name—the Cornhuskers—as suggested by a local sportswriter, Charlie "Cy" Sherman. By the end of his chancellorship the University of Nebraska was the nation's fifth-largest public institution. Nine buildings were also constructed during Andrews's tenure, including the first student activities building and the Temple Building.

### GEORGE EDWIN MACLEAN (1895–1899)

George Edwin MacLean, a professor of English language and literature at the University of Minnesota, was recommended for the post of chancellor by the outgoing James Canfield, and was elected by the Board of Regents as the sixth chancellor of the University of Nebraska in 1895. Under MacLean's watch the University's Latin School was discontinued, a Graduate School was organized, the first scholarships were instituted, and the University Library (today's Architecture Hall) opened.

### JAMES HULME CANFIELD (1891–1895)

Although he occupied the office for only four years, James Canfield was the most consequential leader of the early university. During this period Nebraska entered its first golden age and, along with Michigan, Wisconsin, and California, became one of the "big four" universities of the American West. Canfield was instrumental in the development of the campus environment and undertook a series of improvements that greatly enhanced its attractiveness. Included in these improvements were the addition of paved sidewalks and formal landscaping, the construction of a library—now Architecture Hall—and the installation of a decorative iron fence that surrounded the original city campus until the 1920s.

### CHARLES EDWIN BESSEY (1888–1891, 1899–1900)

Charles Bessey, a professor who did much to lay the foundation of American botany, was first chosen as acting chancellor after Irving Manatt's departure in 1888. He served until the summer of 1891, and again from summer 1899 to 1900, between the chancellorships of George MacLean and Elisha Andrews. Because of the duration of his interim leadership of the University and the fact he was asked to lead not once but twice, Bessey is considered the fourth chancellor of the University of Nebraska. In Bessey's time higher education was undergoing a shift from narrow recitation and memorization of textbook materials to lectures, where a professor synthesized and discussed subject material from numerous sources, to seminars, where professors involved students as near-equals in the examination and discussion of knowledge.

### JAMES IRVING MANATT (1884–1888)

During James Manatt's chancellorship major new investments in buildings were made, including a chemistry laboratory (which would eventually become Pharmacy Hall), Grant Memorial Hall, an armory, a gymnasium, and the original Nebraska Hall. With help from Charles H. Gere, head of the Board of Regents, Manatt moved the University forward with ambition and energy. Manatt also appointed several prominent faculty members during his tenure, including botanist Charles Bessey, chemist Rachel Lloyd, and physicist DeWitt Brace.

### EDMUND BURKE FAIRFIELD (1876–1882)

The Edmund Fairfield era was part of a wholesale revolution in educational reform and the nature of religion and its place in public higher education. A debate sweeping higher education hinged on whether a state university should rest on the "old" foundation of religion and recitation or embrace the "new" foundation of secularism and lecture in teaching. The University of Nebraska, formed at the end of the era of recitation, was an ideal—if quarrelsome—laboratory for change. Although Fairfield clashed with members of the faculty, with the Board of Regents, and with local newspaper writers over these issues, he hired the University's first female faculty member, Ellen Smith, as a teacher of Latin and Greek.

### ALLEN R. BENTON (1871–1876)

Allen R. Benton served as the first chancellor of the University of Nebraska. Though offered a salary of $5,000, Benton declared it too high and accepted $4,000 (equal to the salary of a full professor at Harvard University). A Christian minister, Benton designed the University's curriculum around a classical theme laden with ancient languages and mathematics. Benton was responsible for preparing the first building, University Hall, as well as planning the original four-block campus layout bounded by 10th, 12th, R, and T Streets. Benton significantly shaped the University of Nebraska as it is to this day as a result of his purchase of the plot of land now known as East Campus and the creation of the University seal.

# University of Nebraska Presidents

### HANK M. BOUNDS (2015–PRESENT)

Hank M. Bounds became the seventh president of the University of Nebraska on April 13, 2015. A first-generation college student, Bounds has a demonstrated record of expanding opportunities for students, improving higher education outcomes and efficiencies, and building successful partnerships with policymakers, donors, and business leaders.

### JAMES LINDER (INTERIM, 2014–2015)

James Linder served as interim president of the University of Nebraska from 2014 to 2015. While interim president he also served as president of the University Technology Development Corp. (UTDC). During Linder's tenure University-wide institutes were expanded, a major University fundraising campaign was completed, and the momentum of the University continued to grow.

### JAMES B. MILLIKEN (2004–2014)

James B. Milliken was the first native Nebraskan and first University of Nebraska graduate to be named president of the University. Milliken's nearly ten-year tenure at Nebraska was marked by unprecedented success for the University, including growing enrollment, record levels of research funding, significant physical expansion of the campuses, a highly successful capital campaign, creation of a number of University-wide institutes, an increased commitment to global engagement, and expansion of the University's distance learning programs. The Board of Regents named Milliken president emeritus of the University of Nebraska upon his resignation.

### L. DENNIS SMITH (1994–2004)

During L. Dennis Smith's tenure, which included the completion of the University of Nebraska Foundation's successful $727 million Campaign Nebraska, more than 5 million square feet of facilities were renovated and constructed, including residence halls, classrooms, and research laboratories. Unique public-private partnerships were also created during Smith's service as president, including the Rural Initiative, the Peter Kiewit Institute, and the Center for Biosecurity.

### MARTIN A. MASSENGALE (1989–1994)

Martin Massengale joined the University of Nebraska–Lincoln as vice chancellor for agriculture and natural resources in 1976, and became chancellor of the Lincoln campus in 1981. In 1989 Massengale was appointed interim president of the University of Nebraska and was named president in 1991. Massengale was known as an effective leader and supporter of the concept of integrating research, education, and extension. He also authored or coauthored over seventy scientific papers and was a consultant to several foreign governments.

### RONALD W. ROSKENS (1977–1989)

After serving as chancellor of the University of Nebraska at Omaha from 1972 to 1977, Ronald Roskens was named president of the University of Nebraska in 1977, a post he held for thirteen years. During that time Roskens brought an international perspective to the University by developing programs with universities in Asia, Latin America, Europe, and China. Roskens also negotiated an exchange program with Kabul University in Afghanistan and oversaw development of the Center for Afghanistan Studies at UNO.

### DURWOOD B. VARNER (1970–1976)

Durwood "Woody" Varner became chancellor of the University of Nebraska system in 1970; in 1971 the title of the office was officially changed and Varner became the first person to hold the title of president of the University of Nebraska. Varner served in that position until 1976, a span during which he strongly supported an expansion of the University's academic and cultural outreach efforts. In 1976 he became president of the University of Nebraska Foundation. He led the foundation's first major capital campaign, raising more than $52 million, and spearheaded the fund drive that resulted in the construction of the Lied Center for Performing Arts.

### CLIFFORD M. HARDIN (1968–1969)

From 1954 to 1968 Clifford Hardin served as chancellor of the University of Nebraska, which at that time included the Lincoln campuses, the College of Medicine in Omaha, and extension and research sites throughout the state. Under Hardin's tenure as chancellor the University's enrollment rose from 7,000 to 19,000 students and funding was appropriated for many new University buildings. In 1968 the University of Nebraska system was established and Hardin was named its chief executive officer. Hardin left the University in 1969 to become U.S. Secretary of Agriculture, a post he held until 1971.

# Timeline

**1869**

February 15: The Nebraska State Legislature unanimously approves the charter for the University of Nebraska, to be founded in Lincoln.

The cornerstone of University Hall is laid.

June 3: The Board of Regents holds its first meeting.

**1871**

June 1: Allen R. Benton, former president of Northwestern Christian University (now Butler University) and Mount Union University, becomes the first chancellor of the University of Nebraska.

Four faculty members are hired as chairs of ancient languages, English literature, natural sciences, and mathematics.

September: The University of Nebraska opens.

Students found the Palladian Literary Society.

**1872**

The Industrial College, composed of the School of Agriculture and the School of Engineering, is established.

June 26: The first commencement ceremony is held.

**1873**

Students found the Adelphian Literary Society.

**1874**

June: The Board of Regents purchases the 320-acre Moses Culver farm for $55 an acre to establish a model farm for students. A frame house included in the sale is intended to be a dormitory, but it becomes S. W. "Dad" Perin's home when he is chosen as superintendent of University Farm (now East Campus).

**1876**

Edmund Burke Fairfield is hired as chancellor.

The University confers its first graduate degrees.

Alice M. Frost becomes the first woman to graduate from the University.

**1877**

Ellen Smith is hired as an instructor of Greek and Latin, becoming the first woman appointed to the faculty.

**1878**

George Howard joins the faculty as the first instructor in history.

**1879**

The University of Nebraska Military Cadet Band, the precursor to today's Cornhusker Marching Band, is founded.

**1882**

April 24: Oscar Wilde visits Lincoln and gives a lecture to students, including criticizing the architectural style of University Hall.

Summer: Henry E. Hitchcock is named acting chancellor.

**1884**

Charles E. Bessey is hired as dean of the Industrial College.

January: James Irving Manatt is hired as chancellor of the University. Henry E. Hitchcock steps down as acting chancellor.

**1885**

The chemistry laboratory is constructed. Located on the current site of the Sheldon Museum of Art, the building is renamed Pharmacy Hall in 1919, then razed in 1963 to make room for the Sheldon.

**1887**

The original Nebraska Hall, located near 11th and T Streets, is constructed. The building is deemed unsafe by 1913. The upper floors are removed in 1925, and the building is demolished in 1961.

Grant Memorial Hall is built to serve as an armory. Located in line with University Hall, the building later houses women's physical education classes until it is razed in 1966.

DeWitt Brace joins the University as professor of physics.

March 2: The federal Hatch Act, written with the assistance of Charles Bessey, is passed, enabling "experiment stations" to be established at land grant universities.

**1888**

July: The University Board of Regents, supported by the student body and the Alumni Association, fires Chancellor James Manatt. Charles E. Bessey is appointed acting chancellor and Lewis E. Hicks, professor of geology, takes Bessey's place as dean of the Industrial College.

**1889**

Soldiers Memorial Hall, featuring an auditorium with a pipe organ originally made for Omaha's 1898 Trans-Mississippi Exposition, is added to the west side of Grant Memorial Hall.

Harry K. Wolfe, a native Nebraskan and one of the first two Americans to earn a PhD in philosophy, joins the faculty.

November 23: The University of Nebraska holds its first football game, a contest between seniors and sophomores.

A baseball team and a men's track and field team are established.

**1890**

Nebraska's football team, called the Bugeaters, plays its first season.

The campus's first intramural sports competition—lawn tennis—is held.

## 1891

An iron fence is constructed around the campus to delineate the school area from downtown Lincoln. Smoking and drinking are prohibited within the fence. As the campus grows the fence becomes a hindrance. It is removed in 1925 and placed around Lincoln's Wyuka Cemetery.

The College of Law is established after the University acquires the Central College of Law.

James Hulme Canfield becomes chancellor. He establishes a department of physical education. Nebraska is one of the first universities to offer a degree in physical education for women.

Lt. John J. Pershing joins the University as professor of military science.

December: The Western Interstate Football Association is formed, including the Universities of Missouri, Kansas, Nebraska, and Iowa.

## 1892

George Flippin becomes the first African-American athlete at Nebraska and only the fifth black athlete at a predominantly white university.

Mary L. Jones, who studied under Melvil Dewey, joins the University as "acting librarian" and spends the summer reclassifying the library's collection according to the Dewey decimal system.

Willa Cather becomes literary editor of the *Hesperian*, the student newspaper.

## 1893

Nebraska hires its first football coach, Frank Crawford.

## 1894

A cadet drill team under the leadership of Lieutenant Pershing competes at a national competition in Omaha. The team wins the competition, bringing home $1,500 and the Maiden Cup.

Willard Kimball moves to Lincoln and opens a conservatory of music across the street from City Campus. The Board of Regents purchases Kimball's school in 1930 for $100,000.

Chancellor Canfield hires Carrie Belle Raymond as director of music.

The *Nebraskan*, a second student newspaper, is founded by Frank T. "Rag" Riley.

May 21: The student body votes to censure student Adam McMullen, who tries to represent the University in an oratorical contest using a purchased speech. McMullen went on to serve as governor of Nebraska for one term.

## 1895

Fem. Sem. Bot. is established by female students after they are barred from joining Sem. Bot., an all-male science club.

Five student members and five faculty members form the University board of athletics, establishing rules for all athletic teams at the University.

*Nebraska Literary Magazine*, managed by the English Club, begins its short-lived run of two years.

Chancellor Canfield resigns his position with the University to become president of the Ohio State University. The Board of Regents elects George Edwin MacLean to replace him.

December 10: The University library (now Architecture Hall) is dedicated.

## 1896

August Hjalmar Edgren becomes graduate dean of the first organized graduate college west of the Mississippi River.

The first PhD at the University of Nebraska is awarded to H. N. Allen in physics.

A women's basketball team and women's volleyball team are established.

## 1897

The Dairy Building, used by the Dairy School and located near Holdrege Street, opens. The building is later renamed Agriculture Administration Annex and is eventually razed in 1973.

Roscoe Pound earns the University's second PhD, in plant ecology.

April 26: Chancellor MacLean fires psychology professor Harry K. Wolfe after disagreements over budgetary support for the Psychology Department and the teaching of evolutionary theory. Students protest the dismissal, and Wolfe is rehired in 1907.

A men's basketball team is formed.

## 1898

Professor Rosa Bouton founds the Department of Home Economics.

October 28: Mechanical Arts Hall is dedicated. Constructed on the site of current Manter Hall, it is built to provide classrooms and laboratory space for the growing engineering programs. The building is remodeled several times and razed in 1974.

March: The first women's basketball game against an outside opponent (a team from Council Bluffs, Iowa) is played.

## 1899

The Agriculture Experiment Station Building, now known as Agricultural Communications, is constructed on the southeast corner of the current East Campus mall. This is the oldest remaining building on East Campus.

Roscoe Pound joins the faculty of the College of Law.

June: Chancellor George MacLean accepts an offer to become the president of the State University of Iowa (today's University of Iowa). Charles Bessey again becomes acting chancellor.

## 1900

Elisha Benjamin Andrews is appointed chancellor.

The football team changes its name from the Old Gold Knights to the Cornhuskers, a name first used the previous year by *Nebraska State Journal* columnist Charles "Cy" Sherman. The school changes its colors to scarlet and cream.

**1901**

Miller M. Fogg joins the University and establishes the first debate team. Fogg will become the first director of the School of Journalism in 1917.

The *Nebraskan* changes its name to the *Daily Nebraskan*.

**1902**

Booker T. Washington gives the spring commencement address.

**1903**

The original Dairy Barn is built on East Campus near 38th and Holdrege Streets. In March 1925 the building collapses under the weight of an overloaded hay mow and the barn is demolished.

The Innocents Society is established as a senior honorary society for men.

John D. Rockefeller offers the University $66,666.66 to use in the construction of a student activity center.

Roscoe Pound becomes dean of the College of Law.

**1904**

Construction of Brace Laboratory of Physics begins. The building opens the following year and still stands today.

Construction of Agriculture Hall begins on the East Campus mall. The building opens the following year and today houses the administrative offices of the Institute for Agriculture and Natural Resources.

**1905**

The University's first museum is built, located along the east boundary of campus, near 12th Street. The original design is never completed. The building houses various departments until it is razed in 1970.

Construction of the original Administration Building, located on the site of today's Sheldon Sculpture Garden, begins. The building opens in 1906 and is razed in 1963.

The original Home Economics Building is constructed on East Campus. With the expansion of courses like child development, education, and interior decorating, the space soon becomes inadequate and the building is razed in 1973 to make room for the new home economics facility.

Machinery Hall is built to serve as a classroom, shop, gymnasium, and meat laboratory. Located at the southwest corner of the current East Campus Union, the building is razed in 1964.

An Intra-Fraternity Council is established in response to the regents' fears that the Greek system is too socially focused.

Walter Cowles "Bummy" Booth resigns as University football coach; during his final year Booth's salary was just under $2,000, more than any professor on campus.

Black Masque is established as an honor society for women.

**1906**

Construction of the Temple Building begins, funded by Rockefeller's and private donations. Designed as a space for student activities, the building today houses University Theatre.

An Intra-Sorority Council (now called the Panhellenic Association) is established.

Hays Hall, a privately owned and operated women's dormitory, opens on the corner of 12th and Q Streets, now the site of the Lied Center.

**1907**

The Missouri Valley Conference is organized by the University of Iowa, University of Missouri, University of Kansas, University of Nebraska, Iowa State University, Drake University, and Washington University (St. Louis).

**1908**

Richards Hall (originally called Mechanical Engineering Laboratories), designed by C. R. Richards, then associate dean of the Industrial College, is built.

The Judging Pavilion, used for grain and livestock judging, is constructed. The building is renamed Animal Husbandry Hall in 1932, and renamed again as Miller Hall in 1972.

The Board of Regents establishes Teachers College.

November: Chancellor Elisha Benjamin Andrews resigns due to failing health. Samuel Avery is appointed chancellor.

**1909**

The University of Nebraska joins the Association of American Universities.

The Industrial College separates into the College of Agriculture and the College of Engineering.

Nebraska is ranked fifth in student enrollment among public universities.

**1910**

The University of Nebraska is ranked as the twelfth-largest university in the country and one of the six largest state universities.

A wrestling team is formed.

**1911**

The Associated Women Students (AWS) is founded. One of the largest and most prominent student organizations at the University from 1911 to 1970, the AWS supported and governed female students.

The first women's track and field meet is held, introduced by the director of women's gymnasium, Ina Gittings.

**1912**

A Law College building is constructed at 10th and R Streets. From 1985 to 1987 the building is renovated and linked to Architecture Hall.

The Plant Industry Building is constructed on the East Campus mall.

### 1912 (cont.)

Chancellor Avery recalls the 1912 issue of the *Cornhusker* yearbook due to objections over cartoons in it that criticized the relationship between the state legislature and the University. In response, Avery forms the Student Publications Board to oversee student publications.

### 1913

The School of Commerce, forerunner to the College of Business, is established.

The legislature provides a building fund for the University and land is acquired to expand City Campus from 12th Street to 14th Street and from R to Vine Street, doubling the size of the original campus.

### 1915

The Dairy Industry Building is constructed. In 1972 it is renamed H. C. Filley Hall after a longtime professor of farm management and economics.

### 1916

Bessey Hall, named in honor of Charles Bessey, is constructed, the first building to fall outside the boundaries of the original campus.

Chemistry Laboratory, renamed Avery Hall in 1948, is built to replace the original 1885 chemistry building.

After Indiana offers Nebraska football coach E. O. "Jumbo" Stiehm a salary of $4,500, Nebraska offers $4,250 to retain him. Faculty argue that no coach should be paid more than a professor, leading the University to withdraw the offer. Stiehm resigns.

The first Farmers' Fair is held to promote the College of Agriculture.

Phi Kappa Psi builds the first fraternity house.

### 1917

Construction begins on the Social Sciences Building, later known as the College of Business Administration and Louise Pound Hall (starting in 2018). The partially constructed building is appropriated for use by the Student Army Training Corps in 1918 and completed in 1919.

Varsity Dairy, the precursor to today's Dairy Store, opens.

John G. Neihardt receives an honorary doctorate.

January: The University's Military Department becomes a unit of the Reserve Officers Training Corps (ROTC).

April 6: The United States enters World War I.

April 18: Nebraska Governor Keith Neville signs a bill establishing a Nebraska Council of Defense to monitor any Nebraskans suspected of disloyalty.

April 24: A "Patriotic Convocation" is held and includes a parade around campus of 4,000 faculty members, students, and ROTC members.

May 31: Professor G. W. A. Luckey, graduate dean of the Teachers College, delivers a commencement speech in which he supports neutrality in World War I and quickly comes under suspicion by the Council of Defense.

December: Regent Frank Haller is forced to resign after challenging the Council of Defense.

### 1918

Agricultural Engineering building is constructed; it is renamed L. W. Chase Hall in 1982 to honor the former agricultural engineering professor and department head.

Animal Pathology and Hygiene Complex is built. Only the stable and main building (later the Natural Resources building) exist today.

The University annexes Lincoln Dental College.

Faculty members raise $50,000 and students raise an additional $23,000 during a campus Liberty Loan drive.

Spring: The Council of Defense accuses twelve University professors of disloyalty.

June: The Board of Regents holds "loyalty trials" for accused faculty members. After ten days of proceedings the regents exonerate all of the professors. Five are asked to resign but the demand is later withdrawn.

### 1919

The original Teachers College building is constructed. The Administration Building, constructed in 1957, is joined to the south end of Teachers College and the two buildings are later renamed Canfield Administration Building.

The College of Business Administration is established.

### 1920

The University purchases Ellen Smith Hall, located on the northwest corner of 14th and R Streets, to use for women's social acitivities. Named in honor of the University's former registrar, the building is razed in 1958 despite public protests.

### 1923

Student Harry Pecha writes "Dear Old Nebraska U."

The School of Journalism is established.

April 26: A groundbreaking ceremony is held for Memorial Stadium.

October 13: The first game is played at Memorial Stadium against Oklahoma, concluding with a 24–0 Nebraska victory.

October 20: Memorial Stadium is dedicated on the day of the homecoming game against the University of Kansas. The game ends in a scoreless tie.

### 1924

Mabel Lee joins the University of Nebraska as professor and director of physical education.

### 1925

Construction begins on the Coliseum, the first building placed along a planned

Memorial Mall running east of Memorial Stadium.

**1926**

The College Activities Building is constructed on East Campus for physical education classes and social activities.

June 5: The first commencement ceremony is held at the completed Coliseum.

**1927**

May 28: Morrill Hall is dedicated. The main feature of the building is "elephant hall" housing the ancient elephant skeletons gathered during expeditions funded by Charles Morrill, after whom the museum is named.

The first issue of *Prairie Schooner*, established by English professor Lowry C. Wimberly, is published.

January: Chancellor Avery retires due to poor health. Edgar A. Burnett, dean of the College of Agriculture, becomes acting chancellor.

**1928**

Edgar A. Burnett is elected chancellor by the Board of Regents.

May 19: After a meeting in Lincoln, the Missouri Valley Conference splits, and Nebraska becomes a member of the Big Six Conference.

September: Andrews Hall, named in honor of Chancellor Elisha Benjamin Andrews and which originally housed the College of Dentistry and the Departments of Foreign Languages and English, opens.

A men's cross country team is formed.

**1929**

A men's tennis team is established.

**1930**

The Columns, located between Memorial Stadium and the Coliseum, are erected.

March 26: The first issue of "With Fire and Sword," a scandal sheet presumably written by students and criticizing administration and faculty, appears on campus.

**1931**

March: Chancellor Burnett hires the Pinkerton Detective Agency to expose the authors of "With Fire and Sword." A detective stays on campus for a few months but never discovers the culprits.

**1932**

Chancellor Burnett mandates that all salaries above $1,000 be cut by 10 percent and cuts his own salary by 20 percent in response to the economic depression.

February 13: During the waning years of prohibition Professor Lowry C. Wimberly and a fellow English instructor are arrested for possession of liquor after chaperoning an all-university party where alcohol was present. The Board of Regents suspends both instructors until September 1 in what becomes known as the "Wimberly Affair."

Fall: Carrie Belle Raymond Hall, named after the longtime music professor, is dedicated. It is the first campus dormitory and houses 170 women who paid $60 per semester for a double room.

**1933**

The Perin home on East Campus is demolished.

The Crops Laboratory is constructed for agronomy research. The building is renamed Kiesselbach Crops Research Laboratory in 1969 in honor of faculty member Theodore Kiesselbach.

Fall: The University accepts money from the Civil Works Administration to construct a stadium track.

**1934**

The University allows federal relief money to be made available to students needing financial assistance.

**1935**

The University accepts Federal Emergency Relief Administration financing for improvements to East Campus.

Largely led by student Frank Jackson "Jack" Fisher, students petition the Board of Regents to request Public Works Administration (PWA) funds for the construction of a new student union.

Spring: Led by student Virginia Selleck, students protest the high cost of used books sold at the University-owned bookstore.

A men's golf team is formed.

George Norris receives an honorary doctorate.

**1936**

Chancellor Burnett establishes the University of Nebraska Foundation to act as the primary fundraiser for the University.

November 21: The men's glee club debuts "Hail Varsity" at a student talent competition. Written by music professor Wilbur Chenoweth with words by alumnus Warren Joyce Ayres, the song is so popular that it becomes the official school song by the beginning of the 1937 football season.

January 11: The PWA approves the University's application for funds to build a student union.

**1937**

Construction of the Nebraska Union begins after the University purchases land for the chosen site, which is outside the boundaries of the original campus. The union opens in 1938.

**1938**

July: Due to old age, Chancellor Burnett petitions the Board of Regents for a leave of absence, followed by retirement. The Board accepts his request and hires Chauncey Samuel Boucher as the new chancellor.

**1939**

Fall: Through the Civil Aeronautics Authority the University offers flying instruction to forty students, including three women.

**1940**

Love Memorial Co-op Hall is built on East Campus. A gift from Don L. Love, mayor of Lincoln and prominent University benefactor, in memory of his late wife, Julia, the dormitory is intended as a cooperative living experience for young women.

Two wings are added to Raymond Hall. One is named after Amanda Heppner, then retired dean of women, and the other for Julia Love.

March: Tuition fees increase from $1.50 to $2.50 per credit hour.

**1941**

January 1: The University football team plays in the Rose Bowl, the program's first bowl game. The Cornhuskers lose to Stanford, 21–13.

To provide more room for the Engineering Mechanics Department and laboratory space for teacher training courses, the University purchases Bancroft School, a junior high school that opened in 1915. Bancroft Hall, located near 14th and U streets, is demolished in 2000.

The Food and Nutrition Building is constructed on East Campus. The building is designed to house laboratories, a cafeteria, dining rooms, a kitchen, offices, and classrooms. It is renamed Ruth Leverton Hall in 1976 in honor of the longtime food and nutrition sciences faculty member.

The University of Nebraska Press is founded.

Spring: Groundbreaking for Love Library is held. Don Love, who died in 1940, left a gift of $800,000 for construction of the library, the largest building on campus at the time it is completed in 1943.

December: After the attack on Pearl Harbor, Chancellor Boucher calls a University-wide convocation.

**1942**

Construction begins on Schulte Field House, named in honor of Henry F. Schulte, track coach from 1919 to 1938 and head football coach in 1919 and 1920. Because of war rationing, the building is not completed until 1949. It is razed in 2004.

The University holds a Food for Freedom campaign, sending 1,600 volunteers across the state to teach Nebraskans how to grow their own victory gardens and conserve food.

**1943**

Enrollment drops by one-third as men are drafted or enlist in the U.S. armed services. Corps cadets from across the country and University ROTC members are housed in Love Library.

April: Students in advanced ROTC are called to active duty.

**1944**

November: The Board of Regents reports that the University has housed 13,769 military men and women since 1941.

**1945**

March: Chancellor Boucher informs the Board of Regents that he plans to retire effective September 1, 1946. The Board appoints T. J. Thompson, dean of student affairs, to serve as acting chancellor.

**1946**

Construction begins on Burnett Hall. Originally planned as a companion building to Andrews Hall in 1928, construction was delayed by the Depression and World War II. The building, named after Chancellor Burnett, opens in 1948.

Nine temporary buildings provided by the Federal Works Administration to ease crowding from the rapid enrollment growth after World War II are moved to campus from the Hastings, Nebraska, military base. All of the buildings are removed by 1962.

Construction begins on the Military and Naval Science Building, which opens the following year. The building is renamed the John J. Pershing Military and Naval Science Building in 2006.

Reuben G. Gustavson joins the University as chancellor.

**1947**

The Legislature passes a $1.1 million levy for new buildings at the University.

November: The University student council holds a meeting of all Big Six schools to discuss racial discrimination in sports. The council votes to withdraw from the Big Six unless discriminatory rules are changed.

**1948**

Postwar parking congestion on campus nearly leads to a full-fledged student riot when police use tear gas to disperse students agitating for better parking.

The University makes full health services available to students for the first time.

A men's gymnastics team is established.

**1949**

Fall: Mueller Tower is dedicated during homecoming. The bell tower, a gift from Ralph Mueller, an 1898 alum, still stands on City Campus.

Chancellor Gustavson persuades the Board of Regents to issue a directive integrating the dorms; official nondiscriminatory policies are established.

**1950**

Ferguson Hall, built for the Electrical Engineering Department and named to honor O. J. Ferguson, a retired dean of engineering, opens on City Campus.

Norman Geske becomes director of University art galleries.

**1952**

The Agronomy Building, the first large academic building constructed on East Campus after World War II, is built. The building is renamed Keim Hall in 1967 to honor Franklin D. Keim, a longtime Agronomy Department chair.

**1953**

The Meat Laboratory is constructed. *Nebraska Farmer* called it "one of the finest meat laboratories in the country." In 1967 the building is renamed Loeffel Meat Laboratory to honor professor William Loeffel.

May: Chancellor Gustavson resigns and appoints John Selleck, business manager of the University, as acting chancellor.

**1954**

Clifford M. Hardin becomes chancellor.

Fall: Selleck Quadrangle, a new dormitory complex on 15th Street, opens. Named in honor of John Selleck, a 1912 graduate and longtime University employee who earned the nickname "Mr. University," the dorm originally houses 800 male students.

November 1: KUON-TV Channel 12, only the seventh public broadcasting television station in the nation, goes on air.

**1955**

University High School opens, housing the University's Teachers College training school. The school closes in 1967 and the building is renamed Henzlik Hall (in honor of former Teachers College dean Frank Henzlik) and converted to offices and college classrooms.

The University's first mascot debuts and soon gains the moniker "Corncob Man."

**1956**

A third wing is added to Raymond Hall and is named after Elsie Piper, a retired associate dean of women. Together the wings become known as the Women's Residence Halls. In 1973 the name is changed to John G. Neihardt Residential Center.

**1958**

Nebraska becomes one of the top twenty-five universities according to the Educational Records Bureau. The school is awarded $1.5 million for research and training.

The new Administration Building opens. The building is later renamed Canfield Hall to honor Chancellor Canfield.

The Student Health Center, financed by student fees, opens.

Chancellor Hardin appoints a joint city-University committee to supervise the construction of Sheldon Memorial Art Gallery.

Mueller Planetarium opens in Morrill Hall.

The University purchases the former Elgin watch factory northeast of City Campus. The building is renovated and becomes Nebraska Hall.

**1960**

Construction for the Nebraska Center for Continuing Education begins at the corner of 33rd and Holdrege Streets. The building, which included a hotel, opens in 1961 to host conferences and seminars. Renamed Hardin Hall in 1994 in honor of Chancellor Clifford Hardin, the building is extensively renovated in 2003 for classroom and office use.

**1961**

The editor of the *Daily Nebraskan* urges the abolition of the U.S. House of Representatives Un-American Activities Committee, putting the student editorial board and the College of Journalism under investigation.

**1962**

Construction begins on the Nelle Cochrane Woods Art Building, which opens in 1963.

Mari Sandoz receives an honorary doctorate.

Bob Devaney is hired as head football coach.

April: Arizona senator Barry Goldwater draws 6,000 students to his presentation at the Coliseum.

**1963**

Mary Mielenz is the first female faculty member to be awarded the University's Distinguished Teacher Award.

Construction of C. Y. Thompson Library begins on East Campus. The library is dedicated in 1966 and named in honor of Charles Yoder Thompson, a leader in Nebraska agriculture and a longtime regent.

Because of enrollment growth the University rents four floors of the downtown Capital Hotel for male students needing housing.

May 16: The Sheldon Memorial Art Gallery is dedicated with architect Philip Johnson speaking at the ceremony. The gallery is renamed Sheldon Museum of Art in 2008.

**1964**

University regents officially rename Agriculture Campus East Campus.

Women are allowed to live in Selleck Quadrangle due to a shortage of women's housing on campus. Senior women are permitted to live in apartments off campus.

**1965**

Abel Hall, a dormitory for men named in honor of University benefactor George Abel, opens.

December: Behlen Laboratory of Physics opens. It is named for Walter Behlen, founder of Behlen Manufacturing Company in Columbus, Nebraska, who partially funded the building.

**1966**

Sandoz Hall, named for Nebraska writer Mari Sandoz, is completed and opens as a women's dormitory.

Contracts are accepted for the construction of three additional residence halls: Harper, Schramm, and Smith.

**1967**

Maxwell Arboretum, named after Nebraska Extension forester Earl G. Maxwell, is established on East Campus.

Bob Devaney becomes athletic director while remaining head football coach.

Westbrook Music Building opens. It is named for Arthur Westbrook, who helped create the School of Music.

**1968**

July 1: The University of Nebraska system is formed after the Municipal University of Omaha is absorbed into the University. University of Nebraska–Lincoln, University of Nebraska–Omaha, and University of Nebraska Medical Center are designated as separate campuses. Chancellor Hardin becomes the chief administrative officer of all three campuses and Joseph Soshnik becomes president of UNL.

November: Newly elected U.S. president Richard Nixon appoints Chancellor Hardin Secretary of Agriculture. Hardin takes a leave of absence from the University on January 1, 1969, and formally resigns in June 1969.

The University Archives is established. After merging in 1978 with the Rare Books and Special Collections unit, it becomes known as the University Archives and Special Collections of the University of Nebraska–Lincoln Libraries.

The Women's Physical Education Building opens. It is later renamed Mabel Lee Hall in honor of Mabel Lee, a longtime director of physical education for women at the University.

**1969**

Oldfather Hall opens. The high-rise building is named to honor Charles Henry Oldfather, dean of the College of Arts and Sciences from 1932 to 1951.

The Centennial Educational Program, or Centennial College, a precursor to today's Honors Program, admits its first students.

April: The Afro-American Collegiate Society stages a three-day protest to address underrepresentation of blacks on campus.

October: Around 4,000 students and faculty march from campus to the State Capitol to protest the Vietnam War.

November 14: Broyhill Fountain, built near the Nebraska Union, is dedicated during homecoming week in honor of Lynn Diann Broyhill, a student who died in a car accident on September 8, 1966.

**1970**

The Sheldon Sculpture Garden is created on the west side of the Sheldon Museum.

Lou Crompton, a professor of English, organizes an interdisciplinary course in gay studies, only the second course of its kind to be taught at an American university.

May 4–5: The Military and Naval Science Building is occupied by students protesting the killing of student demonstrators at Kent State University in Ohio.

Hamilton Hall, named for Cliff S. Hamilton, a Nebraska native and longtime faculty member, opens.

Kimball Recital Hall, named in honor of Willard Kimball, opens.

**1971**

January 1: The football team is named the 1970 National Champions, defeating Louisiana State University 17–12 in the Orange Bowl under coach Bob Devaney.

Fall: Cornstock, a music and dance festival on East Campus, is held for the first time. Thousands of students and alumni attend the event annually until it ends in the early 1990s.

The library acquires its one-millionth volume: a rare copy of *The Works of Geoffrey Chaucer*, published in 1542.

January 14: President Richard Nixon visits campus to present the football team and Coach Devaney with its National Championship plaque.

**1972**

January 1: The football team plays its final game under coach Devaney, defeating Alabama 38–6 in the Orange Bowl, to become the 1971 National Champions.

February: James Zumberge is appointed chancellor.

An unused building on North 16th Street becomes a student cultural center.

The Walter Scott Engineering Center, named in honor of the Omaha native and generous supporter of the University, is dedicated.

**1973**

January: Tom Osborne is named head football coach.

The Institute of Agriculture and Natural Resources is established.

Regents Hall opens to house administration offices. In 1985 the building is renamed the D. B. and Paula Varner Hall after the former chancellor and NU President and his wife.

The College of Architecture is formed.

**1975**

As a result of Title IX of the federal Education Amendments Act of 1972, women's cross country, golf, gymnastics, softball, swimming and diving, track and field, and volleyball teams are established from 1974 to 1976.

Manter Hall Life Sciences Building opens, named in honor of Harold W. Manter, a longtime professor of zoology and anatomy who helped establish the field of parasitology.

### 1976

The Board of Regents names Roy Young as chancellor.

The Bob Devaney Sports Center opens. The center is home to basketball, gymnastics, track, wrestling, and the swimming and diving programs. After a major renovation in 2013 it becomes home to the Husker volleyball program.

The Center for Great Plains Studies is established.

May 8: President Gerald Ford gives the spring commencement address.

### 1977

January 17: The new East Campus Union opens.

Terry Pettit becomes head volleyball coach.

### 1978

Chancellor Young initiates the University's affiliation with the National Merit Scholars Program.

### 1979

The men's gymnastics team wins its first team National Championship, the first of five straight National Championship titles.

### 1980

The men's gymnastics team is named National Champions.

### 1981

The men's gymnastics team wins a third national title.

Martin A. Massengale becomes chancellor.

Nebraska ranks at the top of Big Eight Conference schools in the number of intramural activities.

### 1982

The men's gymnastics team is named National Champions.

The women's indoor track and field team wins its first National Championship.

Dick Cavett receives an honorary doctorate.

### 1983

The women's indoor track and field team wins a second national title.

The men's gymnastics team earns a fifth national title.

### 1984

The women's indoor track and field team earns a third National Championship.

### 1985

The School of Journalism becomes the College of Journalism.

August: The first residence hall computer lab opens in Selleck with thirty-two computers and printers.

### 1986

The Honors Program welcomes its first students.

Danny Nee becomes head coach of the men's basketball team.

### 1987

November: Cook Pavilion is completed. The facility is used by varsity sports teams but is also open to any student.

### 1988

The men's gymnastics team wins its sixth National Championship.

### 1989

September: The Lee and Helene Sapp Recreation Facility is completed, named for its benefactors.

### 1990

The men's gymnastics team earns a seventh national title.

The Lied Center for Performing Arts opens. Funded by a grant from the Lied Foundation Trust, the building is named to honor Ernst M. and Ida K. Lied, the parents of Ernst F. Lied, a 1927 graduate.

The Nebraska women's bowling team wins its first National (IBC) Championship.

### 1992

The Nebraska Union parking lot is converted into green space for student activities.

October: Twenty-six emergency phone units are installed on City Campus and ten on East Campus.

### 1993

The Department of Educational Psychology is ranked number one in the country for scholarly publications.

July 1: The College of Fine and Performing Arts is established.

### 1994

The University celebrates its 125th anniversary.

The men's gymnastics team wins its eighth national title.

A women's soccer team is established.

Graham Spanier is named chancellor.

The Center for Grassland Studies is established within the Institute of Agriculture and Natural Resources. The center emphasizes the role of grasslands as a natural resource and enhances the efficiency, profitability, and sustainability of grasslands and turfs.

### 1995

January 1: Under coach Tom Osborne the football team defeats Miami 24–17 in the Orange Bowl and is named the 1994 National Champion.

The women's bowling team wins a second (IBC) National Championship.

The Beadle Center opens on City Campus. The building is named for George Beadle, a Nebraska native and graduate who won the Nobel Prize in Physiology or Medicine in 1958.

December 16: The volleyball team, under coach Terry Pettit, wins its first national title, defeating Texas 3–1 in the championship match.

## 1996

January 2: The football team under coach Osborne defeats Florida 62–24 in the Fiesta Bowl and is named the 1995 National Champion.

The first annual Burr/Fedde/Love Bull Fry, a philanthropic event on East Campus, is held, featuring entertainment, games, and Rocky Mountain oysters. Since its beginning the event has raised over $100,000 for families in need.

James Moeser becomes chancellor.

## 1997

The International Quilt Study Center is established after the donation of nearly one thousand quilts by Ardis and Robert James. Both native Nebraskans, the James family also provide the lead gift for the construction of the current home of the International Quilt Study Center & Museum.

The Nebraska women's bowling team wins its third (IBC) National Championship.

## 1998

January 2: Under coach Osborne the football team defeats Tennessee 42–17 in the Orange Bowl to become the 1997 National Champion.

## 1999

The women's bowling team earns a fourth (IBC) national title.

A women's rifle team is formed.

Kay Orr receives an honorary doctorate.

## 2000

The Esther L. Kauffman Academic Residential Center opens. Construction of the building is made possible by a gift from Carole and Ed McVaney in honor of Carole's mother, Esther Kauffman.

The College of Fine and Performing Arts is renamed the Hixson-Lied College of Fine and Performing Arts in recognition of an $18 million gift to the University of Nebraska Foundation by Christina M. Hixson and the Lied Foundation Trust.

Harvey Perlman is named chancellor.

December 16: Under coach John Cook the volleyball team wins a second national title, defeating Wisconsin 3–2 in the championship match.

## 2001

The women's bowling team earns its fifth (IBC) national title.

The College of Journalism and Mass Communications moves to Harold and Marian Andersen Hall. Both Nebraska graduates, the Andersens are ardent supporters of the University and a free press.

## 2002

Donald F. Othmer Hall, a new chemical engineering building, opens. It is named for the 1924 Nebraska alum who became a prominent chemical engineer and professor at Polytechnic Institute of New York.

## 2003

Mary Riepma Ross Media Arts Center opens. It is named after the Nebraska alumna who provided the estate gift to fund the theater facility.

The College of Education and Human Sciences is created, combining Teachers College and the College of Human Resources and Family Sciences.

## 2004

The women's bowling team wins the first NCAA-sanctioned National Championship, the team's sixth national title.

The University's PGA golf management program begins, one of only eighteen PGA-accredited programs in the United States.

A major athletics building project begins, including the Tom and Nancy Osborne Athletic Complex, Hawks Championship Indoor Center, and additions to Memorial Stadium.

## 2005

The women's bowling team repeats as National Champions, its seventh national title.

## 2006

December 16: John Cook leads the volleyball team to its third national title, defeating Stanford 3–1 in the championship match.

An official University class ring is initiated.

Fall: The University begins offering a minor in LGBTQ/sexuality studies, one of the first programs of its kind in the Midwest.

## 2007

The Nebraska Student Veterans Organization is created.

Tom Osborne becomes athletic director, a position he holds until January 1, 2013.

## 2008

August 29: The Ken Morrison Life Sciences Research Center is dedicated. The building, located on East Campus, is named for Ken Morrison, a longtime supporter of the University who provided the lead gift for its construction.

Alumnus Ted Randolph, son-in-law of Harry Pecha, who wrote "Dear Old Nebraska U," gives the rights to the Nebraska Alumni Association in exchange for two football tickets to one football game each year.

March: The Quilt House, the current home of the International Quilt Study Center & Museum, opens.

## 2009

The women's bowling team earns its eighth national title.

## 2010

The Jackie Gaughan Multicultural Center opens. The building is named for the native Nebraskan who advanced the hiring of minorities in the gaming industry.

The State of Nebraska transfers ownership of the former Nebraska State Fairgrounds to the University.

**2011**

July: Nebraska joins the Big 10 Conference and Academic Alliance.

**2012**

November 16: The official groundbreaking is held for Nebraska Innovation Campus.

October: The Board of Regents gives final approval for establishing the Rural Futures Institute.

**2013**

The women's bowling team wins a ninth National Championship.

Husker Genetics releases Freeman, a new wheat variety well adapted to dryland farming. It is named for Daniel Freeman, the first person to file for a homestead under the Homestead Act of 1862.

The University launches an online grassland management graduate certificate program.

University Archives and Special Collections, the Center for Digital Research in the Humanities, and Computer Operations and Research Services begin a transcription project to digitize thirty-seven thousand pages of Husker yearbooks.

Pinnacle Bank Arena in Lincoln's Haymarket District becomes the new home of Nebraska men's and women's basketball.

The Sheldon Museum of Art celebrates its fiftieth anniversary and is listed in the National Register of Historic Places.

A University-led team of researchers announces the discovery of a new species of sea anemone living under the Ross Ice Shelf in the Antarctic Sea.

**2014**

Hudl company founders Brian Kaiser, David Graff, and John Wirtz—all former students in the Jeffrey S. Raikes School of Computer Science and Management at UNL—provide $500,000 to establish an endowment for student scholarships in the Raikes School.

**2015**

The women's bowling team earns a tenth national title.

A new East Campus Recreation and Wellness Center opens after extensive renovation and expansion of the existing Activities Building.

October 9: Nebraska Innovation Campus celebrates its grand opening.

December 4: The volleyball team, under coach Cook, wins a fourth National Championship, defeating Texas 3–0 in the championship match.

December 15: The John Breslow Ice Hockey Center—the University's first indoor rink—opens.

**2016**

March 28: The Adele Coryell Hall Learning Commons in Love Library is dedicated. The space is named for the alumna whose family provided the leadership gift for its construction.

May: Ronnie Green becomes UNL's twentieth chancellor.

**2017**

August 18: A ribbon-cutting ceremony is held for Howard L. Hawks Hall, the new home of the College of Business. Hawks, a businessman, philanthropist, and regent, helped fund the construction of the building.

Fall: Massengale Residential Center on East Campus opens, named after Chancellor Martin A. Massengale.

December 16: Coach Cook leads the volleyball team to its fifth national title, defeating Florida 3–1 in the championship match.

December 22: Implosion of Cather and Pound Halls, Nebraska's oldest high-rise residence hall complex, occurs at 9:00 a.m.

**2018**

July 16: A new health center facility opens. The 107,000-square-foot, $43.9 million facility is home to the University Health Center and the Lincoln division of the University of Nebraska Medical Center's nursing program. Alumni Ruth and Bill Scott of Omaha provide the lead challenge gift for the facility's construction.

The Willa Cather Dining Complex opens.

Sixteen UNL students earn Fulbright awards for the 2018–2019 academic year, a new record high for the University.

Scott Frost begins his first season as head football coach at Nebraska.

Memorial Plaques commemorating the WWI service of UNL students and Nebraskans are installed on each side of Memorial Stadium's original entrance.

# University of Nebraska Enrollment Numbers (Fall Semester)*

**1917:** 2,763
**1918:** 3,234
**1919:** 4,245
**1920:** 4,411
**1921:** 4,784
**1922:** 5,345
**1923:** 5,651
**1924:** 5,981
**1925:** 6,105
**1926:** 6,124
**1927:** 6,340
**1928:** 6,484
**1929:** 6,535
**1930:** 6,327
**1931:** 5,945
**1932:** 5,413
**1933:** 5,093
**1934:** 5,075
**1935:** 6,230
**1936:** 6,552
**1937:** 6,595
**1938:** 5,752
**1939:** 6,779
**1940:** 6,491
**1941:** 5,823
**1942:** 5,288
**1943:** 3,035
**1944:** 3,265
**1945:** 4,266
**1946:** 9,648
**1947:** 10,153
**1948:** 10,073
**1949:** 9,416
**1950:** 8,033
**1951:** 6,952
**1952:** 6,684
**1953:** 6,771
**1954:** 7,197
**1955:** 7,899
**1956:** 8,425
**1957:** 8,134
**1958:** 8,356
**1959:** 8,411
**1960:** 8,711
**1961:** 9,436
**1962:** 10,401
**1963:** 11,466
**1964:** 12, 901
**1965:** 15,179
**1966:** 17,061
**1967:** 18, 067
**1968:** 19,150
**1969:** 19, 618
**1970:** 20,810
**1971:** 21,541
**1972:** 21,581
**1973:** 21,160
**1974:** 20,892
**1975:** 22,380
**1976:** 22,179
**1977:** 22,256
**1978:** 22,477
**1979:** 22,661
**1980:** 24,128
**1981:** 24,786
**1982:** 25,075
**1983:** 24,789
**1984:** 24,228
**1985:** 24,020
**1986:** 23,899
**1987:** 23,469
**1988:** 23,985
**1989:** 23,926
**1990:** 24,453
**1991:** 24,620
**1992:** 24,573
**1993:** 24,491
**1994:** 23,854
**1995:** 24,320
**1996:** 23,887
**1997:** 22,827
**1998:** 22,408
**1999:** 22,142
**2000:** 22,268
**2001:** 22,764
**2002:** 22,988
**2003:** 22,559
**2004:** 21,792
**2005:** 21,675
**2006:** 22,106
**2007:** 22,973
**2008:** 23,573
**2009:** 24,100
**2010:** 24,610
**2011:** 24,593
**2012:** 24,207
**2013:** 24,445
**2014:** 25,006
**2015:** 25,260
**2016:** 25,897
**2017:** 26,079
**2018:** 25,820

*Accurate enrollment numbers prior to 1917 are unavailable.

# Husker Athletics through the Years

## Huskers in the Olympics

### 1912 Summer Games at Stockholm, Sweden

Lewis Anderson, Track and Field, USA

### 1936 Summer Games at Berlin, Germany

Sam Francis, Track and Field, USA

### 1956 Summer Games at Stockholm, Sweden

Keith Gardner, Track and Field, Jamaica

### 1960 Summer Games at Rome, Italy

Dan Brand, Wrestling, USA

Keith Gardner, Track and Field, Jamaica, Bronze medal

Joe Mullins, Track and Field, Canada

### 1964 Summer Games at Tokyo, Japan

Dan Brand, Wrestling, USA, Bronze medal

Lynn Headley, Track and Field, Jamaica

### 1968 Summer Games, at Mexico City, Mexico

Charlie Greene, Track and Field, USA, Gold medal, Bronze medal

Clifton Forbes, Track and Field, Jamaica

Carol (Moseke) Frost, Track and Field, USA

Lynn Headley, Track and Field, Jamaica

### 1972 Summer Games at Munich, West Germany

Garth Case, Track and Field, Jamaica

Horace Levy, Track and Field, Jamaica

Leighton Priestley, Track and Field, Jamaica

Donald Quarrie, Track and Field, Jamaica

### 1976 Summer Games at Montreal, Canada

John Ebito, Swimming, Nigeria

Bengt Jonsson, Swimming, Sweden

Leighton Priestley, Track and Field, Jamaica

Donald Quarrie, Track and Field, Jamaica, Gold medal, Silver medal

### 1980 Summer Games at Moscow, Russia

Phil Cahoy, Gymnastics, USA (boycott)

Reynaldo Castro, Swimming, Dominican Republic

John Ebito, Swimming, Nigeria

Larry Gerard, Gymnastics, USA (boycott)

Jim Hartung, Gymnastics, USA (boycott)

Merlene Ottey, Track and Field, Jamaica, Bronze medal

Donald Quarrie, Track and Field, Jamaica, Bronze medal

### 1984 Summer Games at Los Angeles, United States

Janet Burke, Track and Field, Jamaica

Reynaldo Castro, Swimming, Dominican Republic

Jim Hartung, Gymnastics, USA, Gold medal

Scott Johnson, Gymnastics, USA, Gold medal

Jim Mikus, Gymnastics, USA (alternate), Gold medal

Merlene Ottey, Track and Field, Jamaica, Bronze medal, Bronze medal

Donald Quarrie, Track and Field, Jamaica, Silver medal

Marcia Tate, Track and Field, Jamaica (alternate)

Angela Thacker, Track and Field, USA

Dennis Wallace, Track and Field, Jamaica

### 1988 Summer Games at Seoul, South Korea

Kevin Davis, Gymnastics, USA

Scott Johnson, Gymnastics, USA

Wendy Lucero, Swimming, USA

Cathy Noth, Volleyball, USA

Merlene Ottey, Track and Field, Jamaica

Sharon Powell, Track and Field, Jamaica

Bill Scherr, Wrestling, USA, Bronze medal

Jim Scherr, Wrestling, USA

Tom Schlesinger, Gymnastics, USA

Wes Suter, Gymnastics, USA

Marcia Tate, Track and Field, Jamaica

### 1988 Summer Games at Seoul, South Korea (cont.)

Denise Thiémard, Track and Field, Switzerland

Bill Trott, Track and Field, Bermuda

### 1992 Summer Games at Barcelona, Spain

Jan Bidrman, Swimming, Sweden

Robert Bonilla, Swimming, Guatemala

Anja Margetic, Swimming, Bosnia and Herzegovina

Trent Dimas, Gymnastics, USA, Gold medal

Lori Endicott, Volleyball, USA, Bronze medal

Penny Heyns, Swimming, South Africa

Mark Jackson, Track and Field, Canada

Karen Kruger, Track and Field, South Africa

Lenka Maňhalová, Swimming, Czech Republic

Támas Molnár, Track and Field, Hungary

Merlene Ottey, Track and Field, Jamaica, Bronze medal

## 1992 Summer Games at Barcelona, Spain (cont.)

Ximena Restrepo, Track and Field, Colombia, Bronze medal
Peter Williams, Swimming, South Africa

## 1996 Summer Games at Atlanta, United States

Therese Alshammar, Swimming, Sweden
Juan Benavides, Swimming, Spain
Robert Bonilla, Swimming, Guatemala
Lori Endicott, Volleyball, USA
Elvira Fischer, Swimming, Austria
Penny Heyns, Swimming, South Africa, Gold medal, Gold medal
José Isaza Chu, Swimming, Panama
Emma Johnson, Swimming, Australia, Bronze medal
Valery Kalmikovs, Swimming, Latvia
Dieudonné Kwizera, Track and Field, Burundi
Lenka Maňhalová, Swimming, Czech Republic
Nicola Martial, Track and Field, Guyana
Frank Mensah, Track and Field, Ghana
Terrie Miller, Swimming, Norway
Helene Muller, Swimming, South Africa
Patricia Nadler, Track and Field, Switzerland
Merlene Ottey, Track and Field, Jamaica, Silver medal, Silver medal, Bronze medal
Julia Russell, Swimming, South Africa
Lori Sippel, Softball, Canada
Balázs Tölgyesi, Track and Field, Hungary
Linetta Wilson, Track and Field, USA, Gold medal
Anna Windsor, Swimming, Australia

## 2000 Summer Games at Sydney, Australia

Therese Alshammar, Swimming, Sweden, Silver medal, Silver medal, Bronze medal
Juan Benavides, Swimming, Spain
Javier Botello, Swimming, Spain
Rulon Gardner, Wrestling, USA, Gold medal
Elvira Fischer, Swimming, Austria
Penny Heyns, Swimming, South Africa, Bronze medal
Valery Kalmikovs, Swimming, Latvia
Matt Lindland, Wrestling, USA, Silver medal
Helene Muller, Swimming, South Africa
Jimmy Pino, Track and Field, Colombia
Merlene Ottey, Track and Field, Jamaica, Silver medal, Bronze medal
Adam Pine, Swimming, Australia, Gold medal, Silver medal
Ximena Restrepo, Track and Field, Colombia
Jelena Stanisavljević, Track and Field, Yugoslavia
Allison Weston, Volleyball, USA
Michael Windisch, Swimming, Austria
Anna Windsor, Swimming, Australia

## 2004 Summer Games at Athens, Greece

Therese Alshammar, Swimming, Sweden
Rulon Gardner, Wrestling, USA, Bronze medal
Stephanie Skegas-Maxwell, Softball, Greece
Sheena Lawrick, Softball, Canada
Nenad Lonćar, Track and Field, Serbia and Montenegro
Priscilla Lopes-Schliep, Track and Field, Canada
Nancy Metcalf, Volleyball, USA
Dmitrijs Milkevićs, Track and Field, Latvia
Merlene Ottey, Track and Field, Slovenia
Adam Pine, Swimming, Australia
Ineta Radēvića, Track and Field, Latvia
Dace Ruskule, Track and Field, Latvia
Adam Stern, Baseball, Canada
Brad Vering, Wrestling, USA

## 2006 Winter Games at Turin, Italy

Curt Tomasevicz, Bobsled, USA

## 2008 Summer Games at Beijing, China

Therese Alshammar, Swimming, Sweden
Brian Duensing, Baseball, USA, Bronze medal
Györgyi Farkas, Track and Field, Hungary
Dusty Jonas, Track and Field, USA
Sheena Lawrick, Softball, Canada
Karina LeBlanc, Soccer, Canada
Priscilla Lopes-Schliep, Track and Field, Canada, Bronze medal
Robin Mackin, Softball, Canada
Dmitrijs Milkevićs, Track and Field, Latvia
Amber Neben, Cycling, USA
Adam Pine, Swimming, Australia, Silver medal
Adam Stern, Baseball, Canada
Brittany Timko, Soccer, Canada
Amy Walsh, Soccer, Canada
Brad Vering, Wrestling, USA

## 2010 Winter Games at Vancouver, Canada

Shelley-Ann Brown, Bobsled, Canada, Silver medal
Curt Tomasevicz, Bobsled, USA, Gold medal

### 2012 Summer Games at London, United Kingdom

Therese Alshammar, Swimming, Sweden
Chelsea Aubry, Basketball, Canada
Ade Dagunduro, Basketball, Nigeria
Jordan Burroughs, Wrestling, USA, Gold medal
Györgyi Farkas, Track and Field, Hungary
Lehann Fourie, Track and Field, South Africa
Jordan Larson, Volleyball, USA, Silver medal
Karina LeBlanc, Soccer, Canada, Bronze medal
Aleks Marić, Basketball, Australia
Chante McMillan, Track and Field, USA
Carl Myerscough, Track and Field, Great Britain
Amber Neben, Cycling, USA
Ineta Radēviča, Track and Field, Latvia
Brittany Timko, Soccer, Canada, Bronze medal

### 2014 Winter Games at Sochi, Russia

Curt Tomasevicz, Bobsled, USA, Bronze medal

### 2016 Summer Games at Rio de Janeiro, Brazil

Therese Alshammar, Swimming, Sweden
Kayla Banwarth, Volleyball, USA, Bronze medal
Jordan Burroughs, Wrestling, USA
Maruša Černjul, Track and Field, Slovenia
Györgyi Farkas, Track and Field, Hungary
Jordan Larson, Volleyball, USA, Bronze medal
Danielle Page, Basketball, Serbia, Bronze medal
Sarah Pavan, Beach Volleyball, Canada
Kelsey Robinson, Volleyball, USA, Bronze medal
Miles Ukaoma, Track and Field, Nigeria

### Coaches

Francis Allen, head coach, USA Men's Gymnastics, 1980, 1992
John Cook, assistant coach, USA Men's Volleyball, 1992
Jan Bidrman, head coach, South Africa Swimming, 1996; assistant coach, Canada Swimming, 2000, 2004, 2008, 2012
Peggy Liddick, head coach, Australia Women's Gymnastics, 2000, 2004, 2008, 2012
Lori Sippel, head coach, Canada Softball, 2008
Mark Manning, assistant coach, USA Wrestling, 1996, 2000, 2012, 2016
Ashley MacAllister, head coach, Puerto Rico Rifle, 2016

## Current Varsity Sports Teams Notable Statistics

### Baseball

- First season: 1889
- College World Series appearances: 3 (2001, 2002, 2005)
- NCAA tournament appearances: 15 (1979, 1980, 1985, 1999, 2000, 2001, 2002, 2003, 2005, 2006, 2007, 2008, 2014, 2016, 2017)
- Conference tournament titles: 4 (Big Twelve: 1999, 2000, 2001, 2005)
- Conference regular season titles: 7 (Big Six: 1929; Big Seven: 1948, 1950; Big Twelve: 2001, 2003, 2005; Big Ten: 2017)
- Academic All-Americans: 21
- Big Eight Player of the Year: Darin Erstad, 1995
- Big Twelve Player of the Year: Jed Morris, 2002; Matt Hopper, 2003; Alex Gordon, 2004, 2005
- Dick Howser Award: Alex Gordon, 2005
- Big Twelve Coach of the Year: Dave Van Horn, 2001
- Big Ten Coach of the Year: Darin Erstad, 2017
- National Coach of the Year: Dave Van Horn, 2001

### Women's Basketball

- First season: 1896; 1974–75 (as varsity sports team)
- NCAA tournament appearances: 14 (1988, 1993, 1996, 1998, 1999, 2000, 2007, 2008, 2010, 2012, 2013, 2014, 2015, 2018)
- Women's National Invitational tournament (WNIT) appearances: 6 (1992, 2004, 2005, 2006, 2009, 2016)
- Conference tournament titles: 1 (Big Ten: 2014)
- Conference regular season titles: 2 (Big Eight: 1988; Big Twelve: 2010)
- Academic All-Americans: 8
- Big Eight Player of the Year: Maurtice Ivy, 1988; Karen Jennings, 1992, 1993
- Big Twelve Player of the Year: Kelsey Griffin, 2010
- Big Ten Player of the Year: Jordan Hooper, 2014
- Big Eight Female Athlete of the Year: Karen Jennings, 1993
- National Player of the Year: Karen Jennings, 1993
- Big Eight Coach of the Year: Angela Beck, 1988
- Big Twelve Coach of the Year: Connie Yori, 2010

### Women's Basketball (cont,)

- Big Ten Coach of the Year: Connie Yori, 2013, 2014; Amy Williams, 2018
- National Coach of the Year: Connie Yori, 2010

### Men's Basketball

- First season: 1897
- NCAA tournament appearances: 7 (1986, 1991, 1992, 1993, 1994, 1998, 2014)
- National Invitational Tournament (NIT) championships: 1 (1996)
- NIT appearances: 17 (1967, 1978, 1980, 1983, 1984, 1985, 1987, 1989, 1995, 1996, 1997, 1999, 2004, 2006, 2008, 2009, 2011)
- Conference tournament titles: 1 (Big Eight: 1994)
- Conference regular season titles: 6 (Missouri Valley: 1912, 1913, 1914, 1916; Big Seven: 1949, 1950)
- Academic All-Americans: 8
- Big Eight Player of the Year: Andre Smith, 1981
- Big Twelve Player of the Year: Venson Hamilton, 1999
- Big Eight Coach of the Year: Joe Cipriano, 1966, 1978, 1980; Moe Iba, 1980, 1981; Danny Nee, 1991
- Big Ten Coach of the Year: Tim Miles, 2014
- National Coach of the Year: Tim Miles, 2014

### Women's Bowling

- First season: 1997–1998 (as varsity sports team)
- NCAA championships: 5 (2004, 2005, 2009, 2013, 2015)
- NCAA tournament appearances: 15 (2004, 2005, 2006, 2007, 2008, 2009, 2010, 2011, 2012, 2013, 2014, 2015, 2016, 2017, 2018)
- IBC national championships: 5 (1991, 1995, 1997, 1999, 2001)
- National Collegiate Bowler of the Year: Kim Berke, 1992; Diandra Hyman, 2000; Shannon Pluhowsky, 2001, 2004, 2005; Lindsay Baker, 2006; Amanda Burgoyne, 2007; Cassandra Leuthold, 2010; Lizabeth Kuhlkin, 2015
- NTCA Coach of the Year: Bill Straub, 2005, 2013, 2017

### Women's Cross Country

- First season: 1975
- NCAA tournament appearances: 26 (1975, 1977, 1978, 1980, 1984, 1986, 1987, 1988, 1989, 1990, 1991, 1992, 1993, 1994, 1995, 1996, 1997, 1998, 1999, 2001, 2003, 2005, 2007, 2008, 2009, 2010)
- Conference team championships: 5 (Big Eight: 1985, 1988, 1989, 1991, 1993)
- Individual conference champions: 1 (Big Eight: Fran ten Bensel, 1991)
- Academic All-Americans: 3

### Men's Cross Country

- First season: 1928
- NCAA tournament appearances: 21 (1962, 1969, 1970, 1971, 1983, 1984, 1985, 1986, 1987, 1988, 1989, 1990, 1992, 1994, 1995, 1996, 1997, 2000, 2001, 2002, 2010)
- Conference team championships: 1 (Big Six: 1940)
- Individual conference champions: 7 (Big Six: Bobby Ginn, 1940, 1941, 1946; Big Eight: Mike Fleming, 1962; Big Eight: Greg Carlberg, 1970; Big Eight: David Iteffa, 1992; Big Twelve: Jonah Kiptarus, 1996)
- Academic All-Americans: 5

### Football

- First season: 1890
- NCAA championships: 5 (1970, 1971, 1994, 1995, 1997)
- Conference titles: 46 (Western Interstate University Football Association: 1894, 1895, 1897; Missouri Valley Conference: 1907, 1910, 1911, 1912, 1913, 1914, 1915, 1916, 1917, 1921, 1922, 1923; Big Six: 1928, 1929, 1931, 1932, 1933, 1935, 1936, 1937, 1940; Big Eight: 1963, 1964, 1965, 1966, 1969, 1970, 1971, 1972, 1975, 1978, 1981, 1982, 1983, 1984, 1988, 1991, 1992, 1993, 1994, 1995; Big Twelve: 1997, 1999)
- Bowl Game appearances: 53 ([by season] 1940, 1954, 1962, 1963, 1964, 1965, 1966, 1969, 1970, 1971, 1972, 1973, 1974, 1975, 1976, 1977, 1978, 1979, 1980, 1981, 1982, 1983, 1984, 1985, 1986, 1987, 1988, 1989, 1990, 1991, 1992, 1993, 1994, 1995, 1996, 1997, 1998, 1999, 2000, 2001, 2002, 2003, 2005, 2006, 2008, 2009, 2010, 2011, 2012, 2013, 2014, 2015, 2016)
- Academic All-Americans: 108
- Big Eight Male Athlete of the Year: Tom Ruud, 1974–75; Dave Rimington, 1982–83; Danny Noonan, 1986–87; Trev Alberts, 1993–94; Rob Zatechka, 1994–95; Tommie Frazier, 1995–96
- Big Twelve Male Athlete of the Year: Grant Wistrom, 1997–98
- Heisman Trophy winners: Johnny Rodgers, 1972; Mike Rozier, 1983; Eric Crouch, 2001

- Big Eight Coach of the Year: Tom Osborne, 1975, 1976, 1980, 1988, 1992, 1993, 1994
- Big Twelve Coach of the Year: Tom Osborne, 1996; Frank Solich, 1999, 2001

## Women's Golf

- First season: 1975–76
- NCAA tournament appearances: 6 (1990, 1996, 2000, 2001, 2003, 2006)
- Conference team titles: 2 (Big Eight: 1976, 1983)
- Individual conference champions: 2 (Big Eight: Rachelle Tacha, 1996; Big Twelve: Sarah Sasse, 2003)
- Academic All-Americans: 1
- Big Twelve Player of the Year: Sarah Sasse, 2003

## Men's Golf

- First season: 1935
- NCAA tournament appearances: 4 (1973, 1978, 1998, 1999)
- Conference team titles: 2 (1936, 1937)
- Ben Hogan Award: Steve Friesen, 1999

## Women's Gymnastics

- First season: 1976
- NCAA Super Six appearances: 12 (1997, 1999, 2000, 2001, 2002, 2003, 2005, 2006, 2007, 2011, 2014, 2018)
- NCAA tournament appearances: 26 (1982, 1983, 1987, 1988, 1989, 1990, 1995, 1996, 1997, 1999, 2000, 2001, 2002, 2003, 2004, 2005, 2006, 2007, 2010, 2011, 2012, 2014, 2015, 2016, 2017, 2018)
- NCAA individual champions: 5 (Michele Bryant, vault, 1990; Heather Brink, all-around and vault, 2000; Richelle Simpson, all-around and floor excercise, 2003)
- Conference team titles: 23 (Big Eight: 1978, 1979, 1980, 1982, 1983, 1987, 1988, 1989, 1990, 1994, 1995, 1996; Big Twelve: 1997, 1998, 1999, 2001, 2002, 2003, 2005, 2007, 2011; Big Ten: 2012, 2013)
- Conference individual champions: 114
- Conference regular season championships: 2 (Big Ten: 2014, 2017)
- Academic All-Americans: 17
- Big Twelve Gymnast of the Year: Heather Brink, 2000; Alecia Ingram, 2001; Richelle Simpson, 2003; Emily Parsons, 2007; Kylie Stone, 2009
- Big Ten Gymnast of the Year: Emily Wong, 2014
- Big Twelve Female Sportsperson of the Year: Richelle Simpson, 2003
- AAI Award: Richelle Simpson, 2005; Emily Wong, 2014
- Big Eight Coach of the Year: Rick Walton, 1987, 1989; Dan Kendig, 1994, 1995, 1996
- Big Twelve Coach of the Year: Dan Kendig, 1997, 1998, 2000, 2003, 2007, 2009, 2011
- Big Ten Coach of the Year: Dan Kendig, 2012
- NCAA Coach of the Year: Dan Kendig, 1999, 2003

## Men's Gymnastics

- First season: 1948
- NCAA tournament appearances: 19 (1975, 1979, 1980, 1981, 1982, 1983, 1985, 1986, 1987, 1988, 1989, 1990, 1992, 1993, 1994, 1995, 1999, 2017, 2018)
- NCAA team championships: 8 (1979, 1980, 1981, 1982, 1983, 1988, 1990, 1994)
- NCAA individual champions: 42
- Conference team titles: 15 (Big Eight: 1964, 1976, 1980, 1982, 1983, 1985, 1986, 1988, 1989, 1990, 1992, 1993, 1994; Mountain Pacific Sports Federation: 1997, 1999)
- Conference individual champions: 99
- Academic All-Americans: 16
- Nissen-Emery Award winners: Jim Hartung, 1982; Wes Suter, 1986; Tom Schlesinger, 1988
- Mountain Pacific Sports Federation Gymnast of the Year: Marshall Nelson, 1998; Jason Hard, 1999; Derek Leiter, 2000; Grant Clinton, 2002
- NCAA Coach of the Year: Francis Allen, 1979, 1980, 1981
- Mountain Pacific Sports Federation Coach of the Year: Francis Allen, 1999
- National Coach of the Year: Francis Allen, 1979, 1980, 1981, 1982, 1983, 1988, 1990, 1994

## Women's Rifle

- First season: 1998–99
- NCAA tournament team appearances: 14 (2000, 2001, 2004, 2005, 2006, 2007, 2008, 2010, 2013, 2014, 2015, 2016, 2017, 2018)
- NCAA individual champions: 3 (Nicole Allaire, smallbore, 2000; Kristina Fehlings, air rifle, 2006; Rachel Martin, smallbore, 2015)

## Women's Rifle (cont.)

- Conference tournament titles: 2 (Great America Rife Conference: 2005, 2006)
- Academic All-Americans: 3
- Collegiate Rifle Coaches Association Coach of the Year: Karen Anthony, 2000; Stacy Underwood, 2014

## Women's Soccer

- First season: 1994
- NCAA tournament appearances: 12 (1996, 1997, 1998, 1999, 2000, 2001, 2002, 2003, 2004, 2005, 2013, 2016)
- Conference tournament titles: 6 (Big Twelve: 1996, 1998, 1999, 2000, 2002; Big Ten: 2013)
- Conference regular season titles: 4 (Big Twelve: 1996, 1999, 2000; Big Ten: 2013)
- Academic All-Americans: 5
- Big Twelve Player of the Year: Morgan Malborough, 2009, 2010; Brittany Timko, 2004, 2005, 2006; Christine Latham, 2000, 2001; Sharolta Nonen, 1999; Kim Engesser, 1998; Kari Uppinghouse, 1996
- Big Ten Player of the Year: Ari Romero, 2013; Jordan Jackson, 2013
- NSCAA National Coach of the Year: John Walker, 1996
- Big Twelve Coach of the Year: John Walker, 1996, 1999
- Big Ten Coach of the Year: John Walker, 2013

## Women's Softball

- First season: 1976; first season as NCAA-sanctioned sport: 1982
- Women's College World Series appearances: 7 (1982, 1984, 1987, 1988, 1998, 2002, 2013)
- NCAA tournament appearances: 24 (1982, 1984, 1987, 1988, 1995, 1996, 1997, 1998, 1999, 2000, 2001, 2002, 2003, 2004, 2005, 2006, 2007, 2009, 2010, 2011, 2013, 2014, 2015, 2016)
- Conference titles (postseason): 9 (Big Eight: 1982, 1984, 1985, 1986, 1987, 1988; Big Twelve: 1998, 2000, 2004)
- Conference titles (regular season): 10 (Big Eight: 1982, 1984, 1985, 1986, 1987, 1988; Big Twelve: 1998, 2001, 2004; Big Ten: 2014)
- Academic All-Americans: 30
- Honda Award winner: Denise Day, 1985
- Big Eight Player of the Year: Ali Viola, 1995
- Big Twelve Player of the Year: Ali Viola, 1998; Peaches James, 2004
- Big Eight Coach of the Year: Rhonda Revelle, 1995
- Big Twelve Coach of the Year: Rhonda Revelle, 1998, 2000
- Big Ten Coach of the Year: Rhonda Revelle, 2014

## Women's Swimming and Diving

- First season: 1974–75 (as varsity sports team)
- NCAA tournament appearances: 20 (1985, 1986, 1987, 1988, 1989, 1990, 1991, 1992, 1993, 1994, 1995, 1996, 1997, 1998, 1999, 2000, 2001, 2006, 2016, 2017)
- NCAA individual champions: 1 (Peggy Heyns, 1996)
- Conference team titles: 10 (Big Eight: 1985, 1986, 1987, 1990, 1991, 1994, 1995, 1996; Big Twelve: 1997, 1998)
- Conference individual titles: 145
- Academic All-Americans: 2
- Big Eight Female Athlete of the Year: Penny Heyns, 1995, 1996
- Big Twelve Swimmer of the Year: Julia Russell, 1996
- Western Athletic Conference Coach of the Year: Pablo Morales, 2000
- Big Twelve Coach of the Year: Pablo Morales, 2004

## Women's Tennis

- First season: 1976
- NCAA tournament appearances: 6 (2005, 2006, 2010, 2011, 2012, 2013)
- Conference team titles: 3 (Big Eight: 1977, 1978; Big Ten: 2013)
- Conference doubles champions: 1 (Big Twelve: 2008)
- Academic All-Americans: 3
- Big Ten Female Tennis Athlete of the Year: Mary Weatherholt, 2012, 2013
- Big Twelve Coach of the Year: Scott Jacobson, 2005, 2010
- Big Ten Coach of the Year: Scott Jacobson (co-coach), 2012

## Men's Tennis

- First season: 1929
- NCAA tournament appearances: 10 (Singles: 1987, 1988, 1989, 1990, 1991, 1992, 1993, 2002; Doubles: 1984, 1989, 1990, 1993, 2012)
- Conference singles champions: 1 (Big Eight: 1993)
- Conference doubles champions: 4 (Big Eight: 1990, 1993; Big Twelve: 1996, 2015)
- Academic All-Americans: 2

## Women's Track and Field

- First season: 1911; 1976 (as varsity sports team)
- NCAA team indoor titles: 3 (1982, 1983, 1984)
- NCAA individual indoor titles: 22
- NCAA individual outdoor titles: 31
- Conference team indoor championships: 24 (Big Eight: 1980, 1981, 1982, 1983, 1984, 1985, 1986, 1987, 1988, 1989, 1990, 1991, 1992, 1993, 1994, 1995, 1996; Big Twelve: 1997, 2000, 2001, 2004, 2005, 2011; Big Ten: 2012)
- Conference team outdoor championships: 18 (Big Eight: 1980, 1981, 1982, 1983, 1984, 1985, 1986, 1987, 1988, 1989, 1990, 1991, 1992, 1993, 1994, 1995; Big Twelve: 2000, 2005)
- Conference individual indoor champions: 182
- Conference individual outdoor champions: 190
- Academic All-Americans: 28
- Big Twelve Coach of the Year Indoor: Gary Pepin, 1997, 1998, 2000, 2001, 2004, 2011
- Big Twelve Coach of the Year Outdoor: Gary Pepin, 2000, 2005
- Big Ten Coach of the Year Indoor: Gary Pepin, 2012

## Men's Track and Field

- First season: 1889
- NCAA individual indoor titles: 21
- NCAA individual outdoor titles: 20
- Conference team indoor championships: 37 (Missouri Valley: 1925, 1926; Big Six: 1930, 1931, 1932, 1933, 1936, 1937, 1938, 1940, 1941, 1942; Big Seven: 1949, 1951; Big Eight: 1963, 1972, 1973, 1978, 1985, 1987, 1988, 1989, 1992, 1994, 1995, 1996; Big Twelve: 1997, 1998, 2000, 2001, 2002, 2003, 2004, 2005, 2007; Big Ten: 2015, 2016)
- Conference team outdoor championships: 29 (Missouri Valley: 1921, 1922, 1923, 1924, 1926; Big Six: 1929, 1932, 1933, 1936, 1937, 1939, 1940, 1941, 1942; Big Seven: 1950; Big Eight: 1966, 1987, 1989, 1990, 1995, 1996; Big Twelve: 1998, 2000, 2002, 2004, 2009, 2010; Big Ten: 2013, 2016)
- Conference individual indoor champions: 267
- Conference individual outdoor champions: 296
- Academic All-Americans: 31
- Big Twelve Coach of the Year Indoor: Gary Pepin, 1997, 1998, 2001, 2002, 2003, 2004, 2005, 2007
- Big Twelve Coach of the Year Outdoor: Gary Pepin, 1998, 2000, 2002, 2004, 2009, 2010
- Big Ten Coach of the Year Indoor: Gary Pepin, 2015, 2016
- Big Ten Coach of the Year Outdoor: Gary Pepin, 2013, 2016

## Volleyball

- First season: 1896; 1975 (as varsity sports team)
- NCAA championships: 5 (1995, 2000, 2006, 2015, 2017)
- NCAA tournament appearances: 36 (1982, 1983, 1984, 1985, 1986, 1987, 1988, 1989, 1990, 1991, 1992, 1993, 1994, 1995, 1996, 1997, 1998, 1999, 2000, 2001, 2002, 2003, 2004, 2005, 2006, 2007, 2008, 2009, 2010, 2011, 2012, 2013, 2014, 2015, 2016, 2017)
- Conference titles: 34 (Big Eight: 1976, 1977, 1978, 1979, 1980, 1981, 1982, 1983, 1984, 1985, 1986, 1987, 1988, 1989, 1990, 1991, 1992, 1994, 1995; Big Twelve: 1996, 1998, 1999, 2000, 2001, 2002, 2004, 2005, 2006, 2007, 2008, 2010; Big Ten: 2011, 2016, 2017)
- Academic All-Americans: 38
- Big Eight Player of the Year: Lori Endicott, 1987, 1988; Virginia Stahr, 1989; Val Novak, 1990; Stephanie Thater, 1991, 1992; Nikki Stricker, 1993; Allison Weston, 1994, 1995
- Big Twelve Player of the Year: Lisa Reitsma, 1996; Fiona Nepo, 1998; Greichaly Cepero, 2000; Nancy Metcalf, 2001; Sarah Pavan, 2005, 2006, 2007; Jordan Larson, 2008
- Big Ten Player of the Year: Kelsey Robinson, 2013
- Big Twelve Co-Players of the Year: Greichaly Cepero, Amber Holmquist, Laura Pilakowski, 2002
- Honda Award winners: Greichaly Cepero, 2000; Sarah Pavan, 2006
- Honda-Broderick Cup winner: Sarah Pavan, 2006
- AVCA National Player of the Year: Allison Weston, 1995; Greichaly Cepero, 2000; Christina Houghtelling, 2005; Sarah Pavan, 2006
- Big Eight Coach of the Year: Terry Pettit, 1985, 1986, 1987, 1989, 1990, 1994, 1995
- Big Twelve Coach of the Year: Terry Pettit, 1996, 1998; John Cook, 2001, 2005, 2008, 2010
- Big Ten Coach of the Year: John Cook, 1997, 2016, 2017
- AVCA National Coach of the Year: Terry Pettit, 1986, 1994; John Cook, 2000, 2005

### Women's Beach Volleyball

- First season: 2013

### Wrestling

- First season: 1910
- NCAA individual champions: 11 (Mike Nissen, 1963; Jim Scherr, 1984; Bill Scherr, 1984; Jason Kelber, 1991; Tony Purler, 1993; Tolly Thompson, 1995; Brad Vering, 2000; Jason Powell, 2004; Paul Donahoe, 2007; Jason Burroughs, 2009, 2011)
- Conference team championships: 7 (WIAA: 1911, 1915; Missouri Valley: 1924; Big Seven: 1949; Big Eight: 1993, 1995; Big Twelve: 2009)
- Conference individual champions: 63
- Academic All-Americans: 7
- Hodge Trophy Winner: Jordan Burroughs, 2011
- Dan Gable Coach of the Year: Mark Manning, 2009
- Big Twelve Coach of the Year: Mark Manning, 2008, 2009

# Acknowledgments

Many thanks to my husband, Tom White, a graduate of the College of Wooster and adopted Cornhusker, for giving up his home office for six months. Thanks to my late parents, Keay Hachiya and Meredith Hachiya DuBois, for choosing to attend the University of Nebraska and remaining in the state their entire lives, establishing my Husker bona fides.

Thank you to Mike Zeleny, a person with endless powers of persuasion, and Meg Lauerman, co-chair with Mike of the N150 celebration. Thanks also to the University of Nebraska Press, including Donna Shear, Bridget Barry, Emily Wendell, Annie Shahan, Ann Baker, and Veronica Duran, as well as research assistants Madhumita Gupta and Dominic Yarabe. Special appreciation to photography director Craig Chandler, and photographers Brett Hampton, Troy Fedderson, Greg Nathan, Tom Slocum, Morgan Spiehs, Erik Stenbakken, and James Wooldridge.

Thank you to contributing writers Monica Norby and Michelle Tilley; and grateful kudos to helpful resources: Beth Burke, Patricia Crew, Barbara DiBernard, Mary Ellen Ducey, Troy Fedderson, Amy Goodburn, Priscilla Grew, John J. Janovy Jr., Emily Levine, Kay Logan-Peters (who really is an expert in all things Nebraska), Marty Ramirez, Guy Reynolds, Kelly Helm Smith, Ann Tschetter, Ken Vogel, Annette Wetzel, Tom White, Kirstin Wilder, David Wilson, and Kevin Wright.

—KIM HACHIYA

UNIVERSITY OF NEBRASKA 2017 COMMENCEMENT
PinnacleBank

PinnacleBank Arena
UNIVERSITY OF NEBRASKA
2017 COMMENCEMENT
UNIVERSITY OF NEBRASKA